The KnowHow Book of Flying Models

Models designed by
Derek Beck
Edited by
Mary Jean McNeil
Educational Adviser
Frank Blackwell

Illustrated by
Colin King
Designed by
John Jamieson

First published in 1975
Usborne Publishing Ltd
20 Garrick Street
London WC2E 9BJ

© Usborne Publishing Ltd
1975

Printed in Great Britain by
Purnell & Sons Ltd
Bristol

About this Book

The aeroplanes in this book are all made from paper and card. The pictures of the aeroplanes show coloured models. You may want to leave your models uncoloured. If you want to colour them as we have shown, use Magic Marker, not paints. For some aeroplanes in this book you will need to use the patterns on pages 42–45. For the planes which need gluing, use quick-drying, powerful glue such as UHU or Bostik 1.

We have used the words 'paper' and 'card' and 'thick card' in this book.

Paper means any normal writing paper, not newspaper.

Card means any thin card about the thickness of a postcard, although actual postcards will be too small. You may use old card folders. If you have to buy them, ask at a stationer for a document folder or square cut folder.

Thick card means really stiff strong card such as the card you find on the back of some writing pads and calendars.

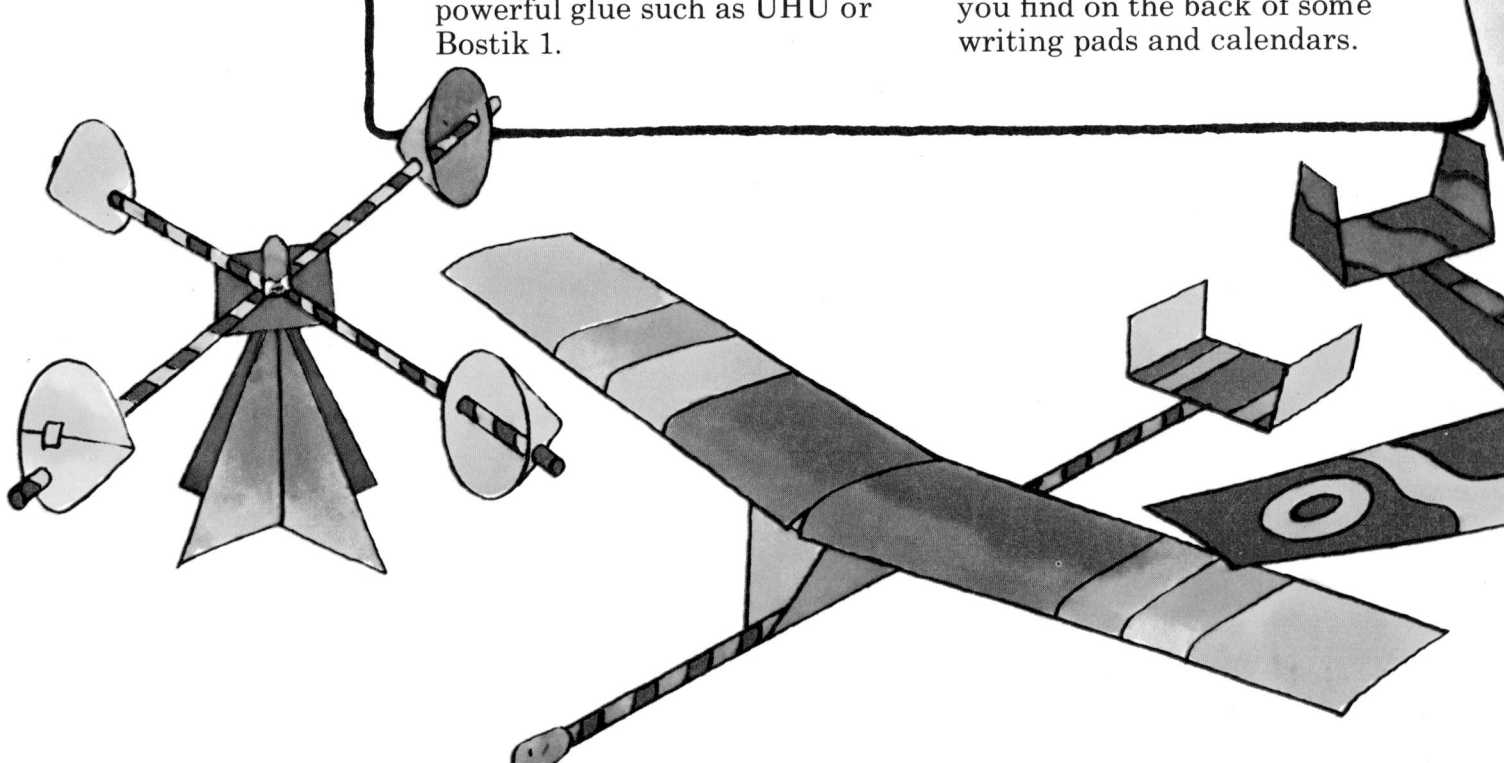

The KnowHow Book of Flying Models

Contents

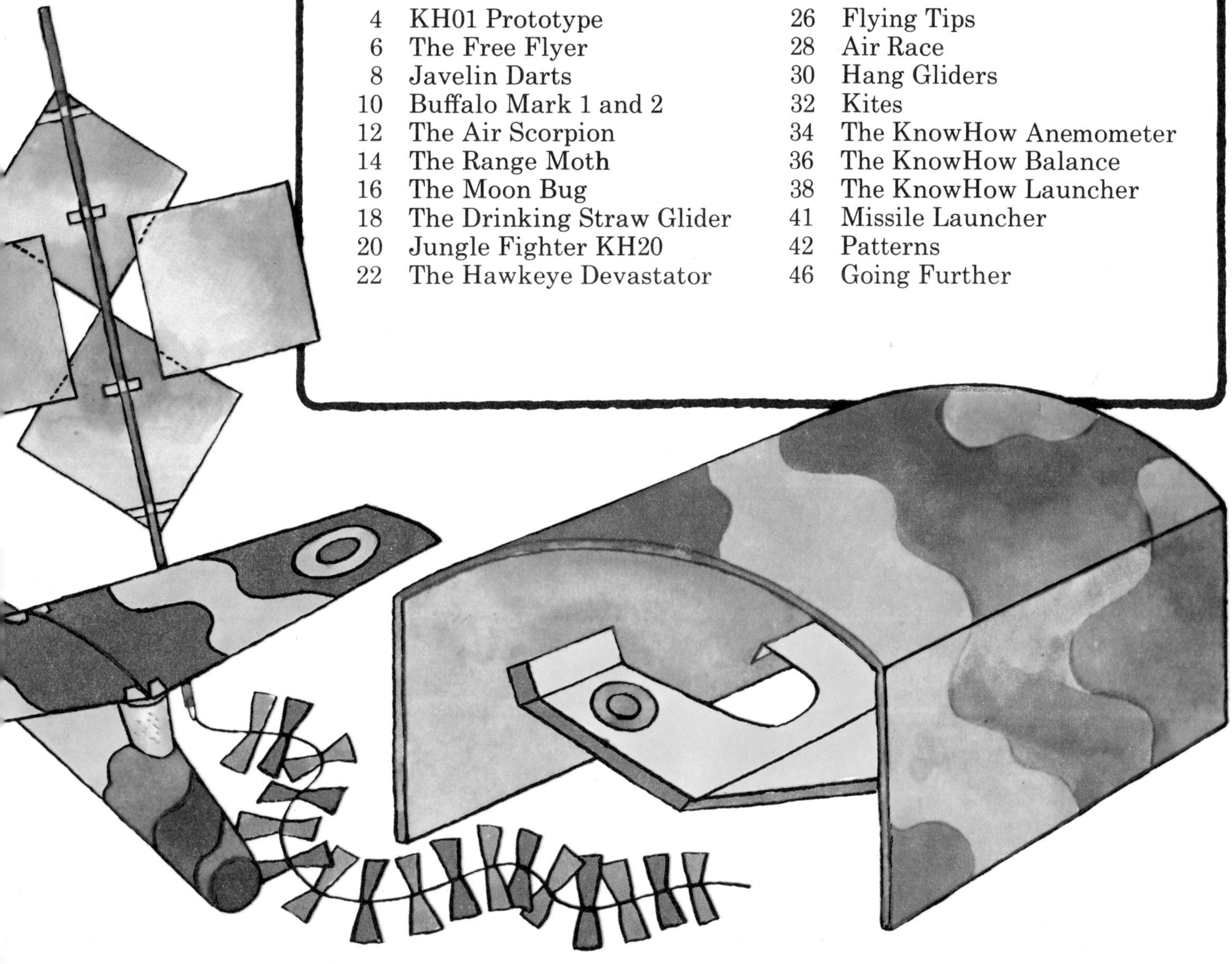

KH01 Prototype

The KH01 Prototype is a very easy plane to make. You can make it from a sheet of paper 21cm × 29cm. Ask for A4 paper. If you cannot make it fly properly, look at the Flying Boxes in the middle of this page. You can find out how to launch it on the next page.

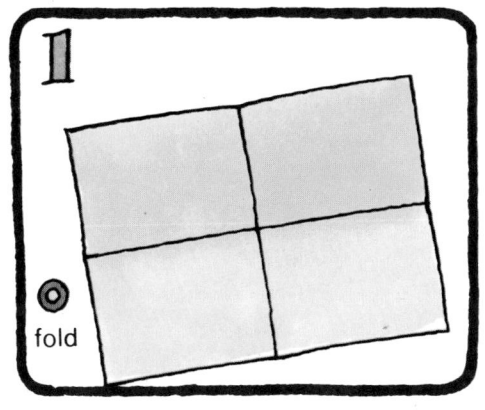

1 fold

Fold a piece of paper exactly down the middle. Unfold it. Fold it exactly down the middle in the other direction. These folds are your guide lines.

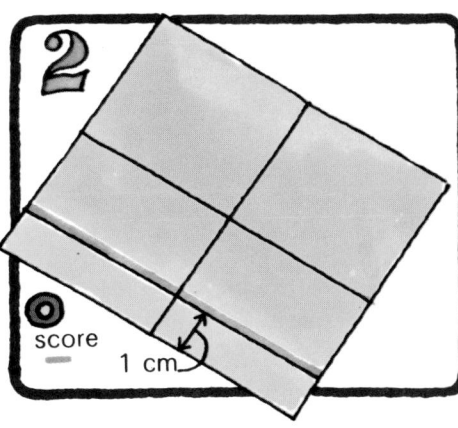

2 score 1 cm

Score a line 1 cm from the long edge of the paper. Then fold the paper up along this line as shown.

If it Stalls

paper clip

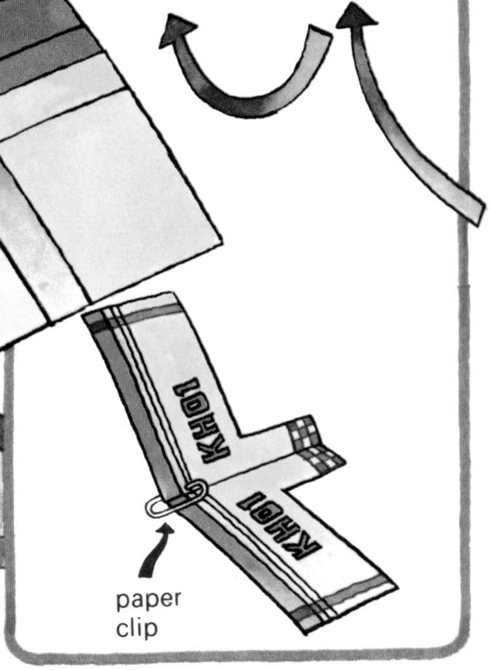

Planes can fly badly in lots of different ways. Sometimes they stall. A stalling plane goes up and down and up and down like this. It stalls because its nose is not heavy enough. Put a paper clip on its front like this. Launch it. If it still stalls put on another one. Or try putting a bit of tape along the folded edge.

The KH01 Prototype

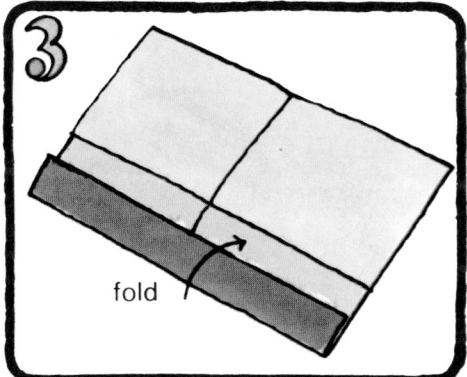

3 fold

Fold the paper again and again until your folded edge reaches the middle guide line.

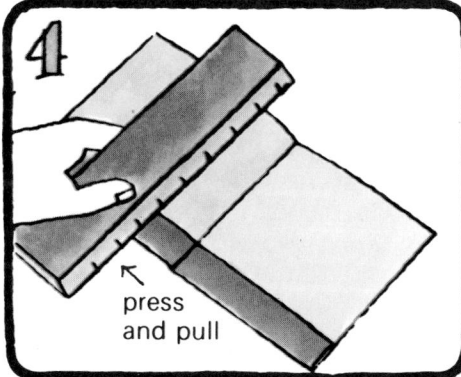

4 press and pull

The last fold has to be really tight, so press your ruler down hard on the paper and run it along the edge.

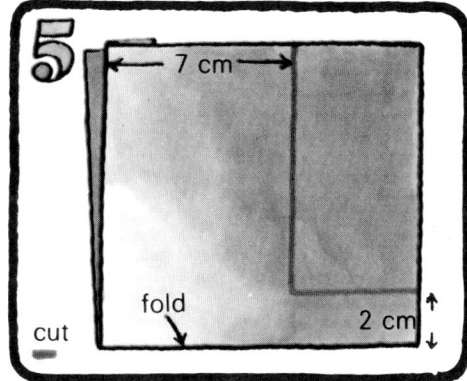

5 7 cm · fold · cut · 2 cm

Fold the paper in half with the folded paper on the inside. Draw and cut out the aeroplane shape as shown.

If it Dives

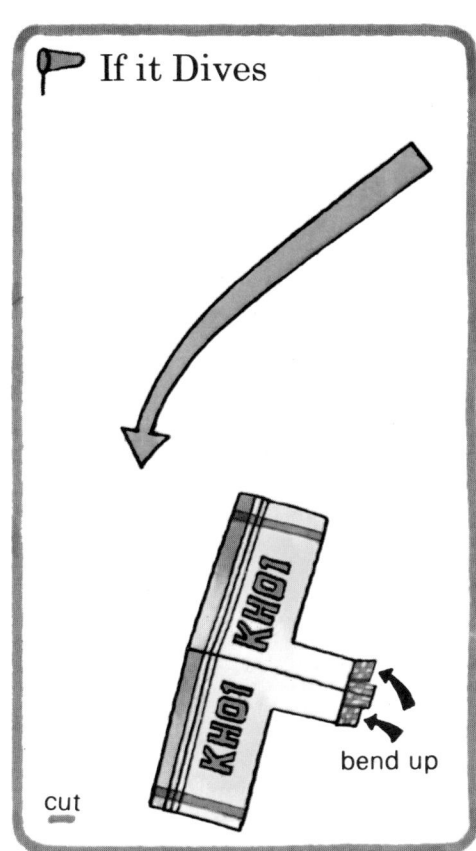

bend up

cut

Your plane may dive nose first to the ground. This may mean that the nose is too heavy. Or it may mean that the tail is not working properly. Make a small cut each side of the tail and bend the paper up as shown. Launch it again. If it still dives, bend the paper up a bit more. Keep doing this until the plane glides smoothly.

Aeroplanes

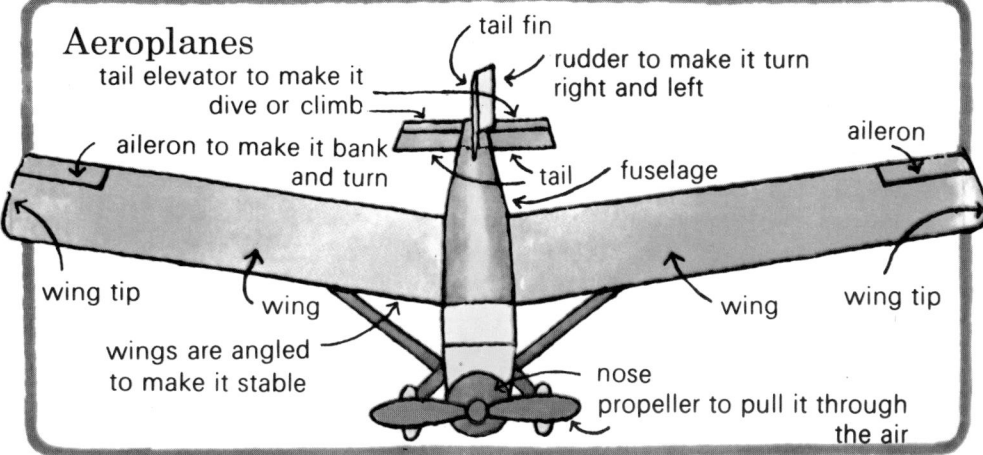

tail fin
tail elevator to make it dive or climb
rudder to make it turn right and left
aileron to make it bank and turn
aileron
tail
fuselage
wing tip
wing
wing
wing tip
wings are angled to make it stable
nose
propeller to pull it through the air

Aeroplanes have lots of different parts. Each part has its own special job.

Look at the aeroplane here and see where the parts are and what they do.

Folding Paper in Half

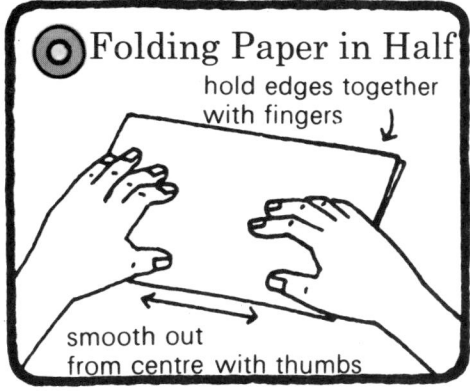

hold edges together with fingers

smooth out from centre with thumbs

For paper aeroplanes, paper folds must be really accurate. The best way is to hold the edges together with your fingers while you smooth the fold down with your thumbs.

Scoring

Lay the paper on something hard and flat. Put your ruler along the line you want to score. Rule a line with a ball point pen. Press the pen down hard all the time.

The Free Flyer

The Free Flyer flies through the air in a very smooth, slow glide. You can make it from a sheet of paper 21cm × 29cm (A4 paper). On this page you will find out how to launch it properly and how to make it turn left and right. All flattish planes like the Free Flyer are launched in this way.

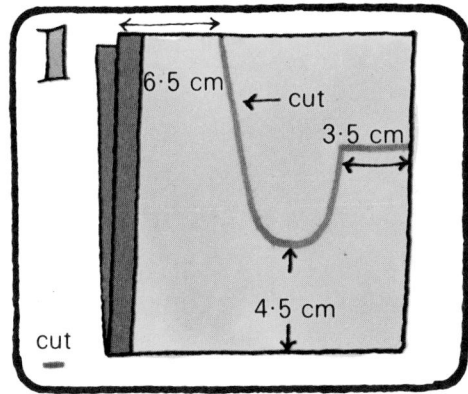

Follow boxes one to four for the KH01 Prototype. Then fold the paper in half with the folded edge on the outside. Draw and cut out the Free Flyer shape as shown.

Score a line 1 cm from the tips of the wings. Bend the top wing edge over the score line and bend the bottom one over in the opposite direction as shown.

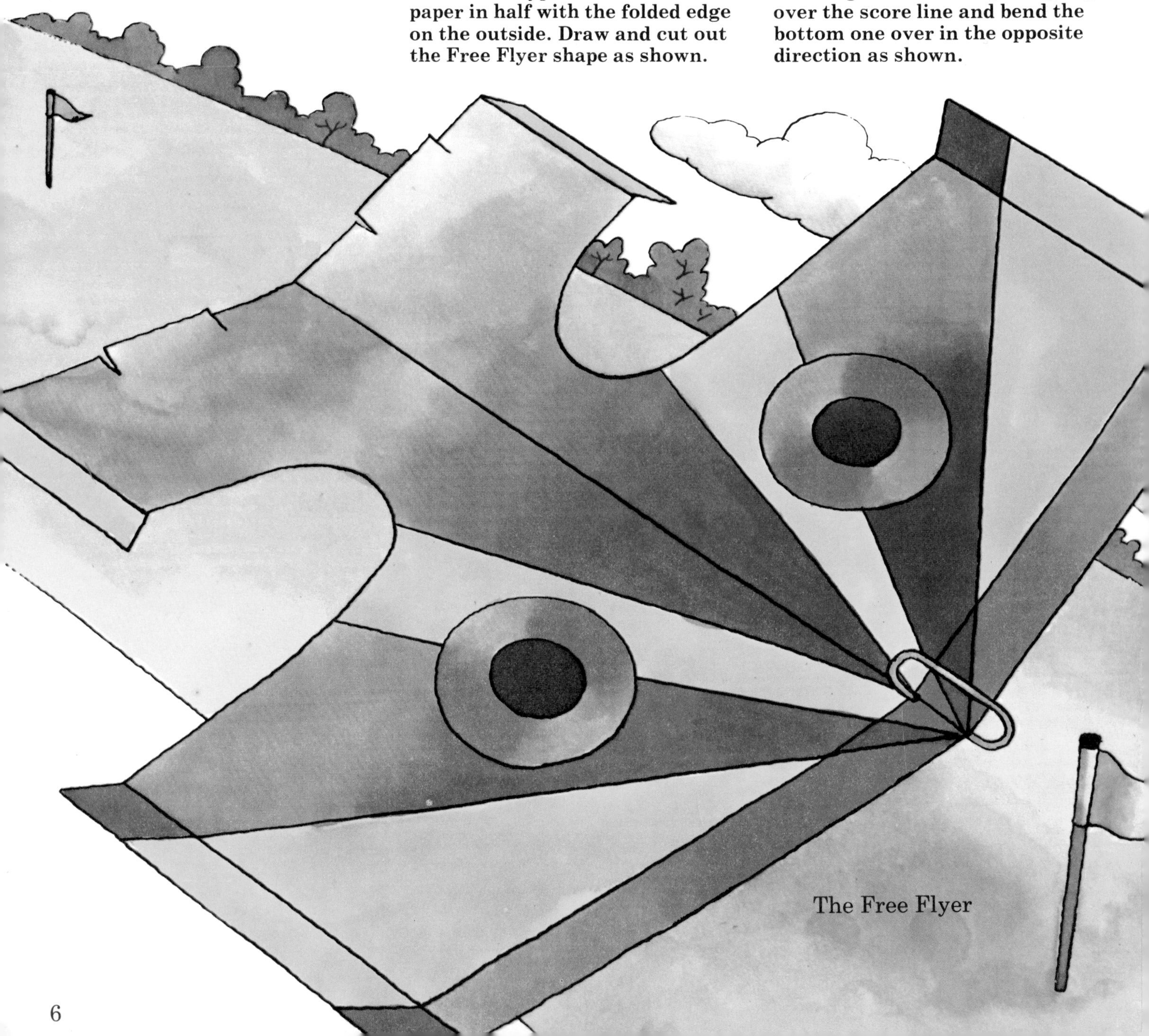

The Free Flyer

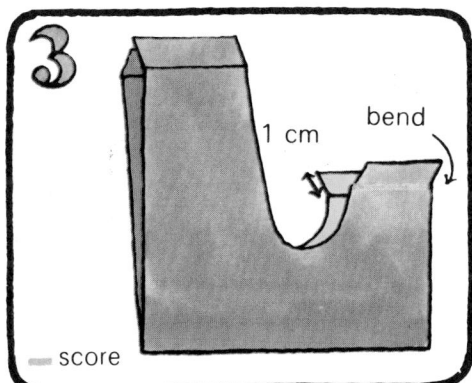

3 1 cm · bend · score

Fold the plane the other way. Score a line 1 cm from the tip of the tail as shown. Bend the tail tips over the score line in opposite directions to each other.

bend down

Bend the back wing edges down by running them between your thumb and fingers. This will curve the wing edge and the plane will fly better. It is called cambering.

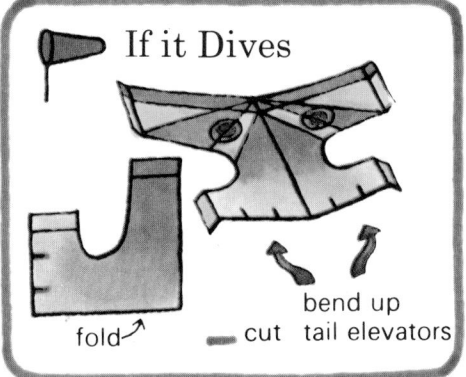

If it Dives

fold · cut · bend up tail elevators

Fold the plane and make two snips in the tail as shown. Unfold the plane. Bend them up until the plane flies smoothly. These are called tail elevators.

Launching a Free Flyer

Put your fore-finger on top of the plane like this with your thumb and other fingers underneath. Point the plane in the direction you want it to go.

Move your hand forward at the speed you think it will fly at and just let it go. Do not jerk or push it forward. Just let it glide from your hand.

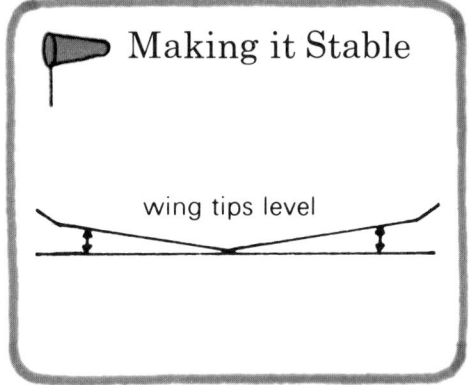

Making it Stable

wing tips level

An unstable plane will spin and somersault to the ground. Hold it up like this. Make sure that the wing tips are level. Push them up or down to make them level.

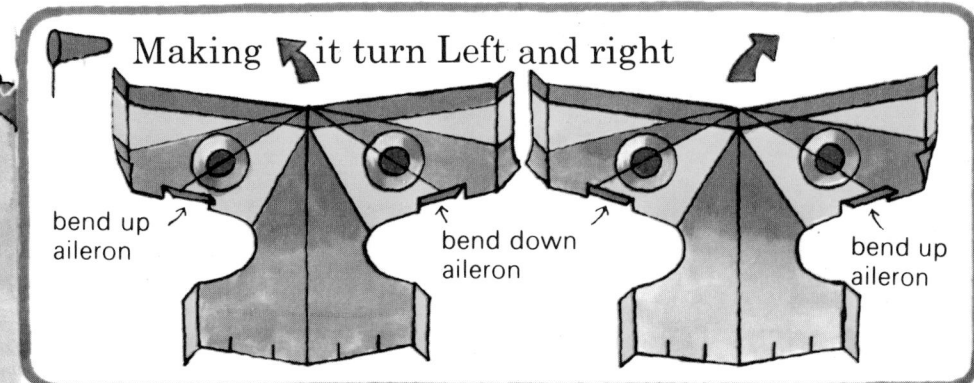

Making it turn Left and right

bend up aileron · bend down aileron · bend up aileron

If you want to, you can make the Free Flyer fly in different directions. Make two little cuts in the back of the wings as shown, to make ailerons.

To make it go left, bend the left aileron up and the right aileron down. To make it go right, bend the right aileron up and the left one down.

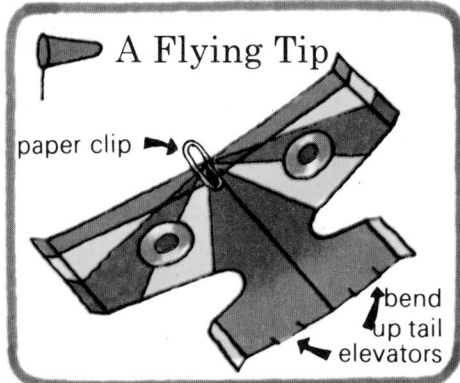

A Flying Tip

paper clip · bend up tail elevators

The Free Flyer will fly very well if you put a paper clip on its nose and bend the tail elevators up a bit.

Javelin Darts

Javelin Darts can be made from a sheet of paper 21cm × 29cm (A4). They fly through the air like arrows. Launch a Javelin hard and it will fly a long way. You should not have to adjust it much. If you want to, you can give it wing tips, but most darts do not have them.

1 fold

Fold the paper exactly down the middle (page 5). Unfold it and put it down on a table like this.

2 fold fold

a b

Fold one of the corners over as far as the centre fold (a). Make sure that it meets the fold exactly. Then fold the other corner over in the same way (b).

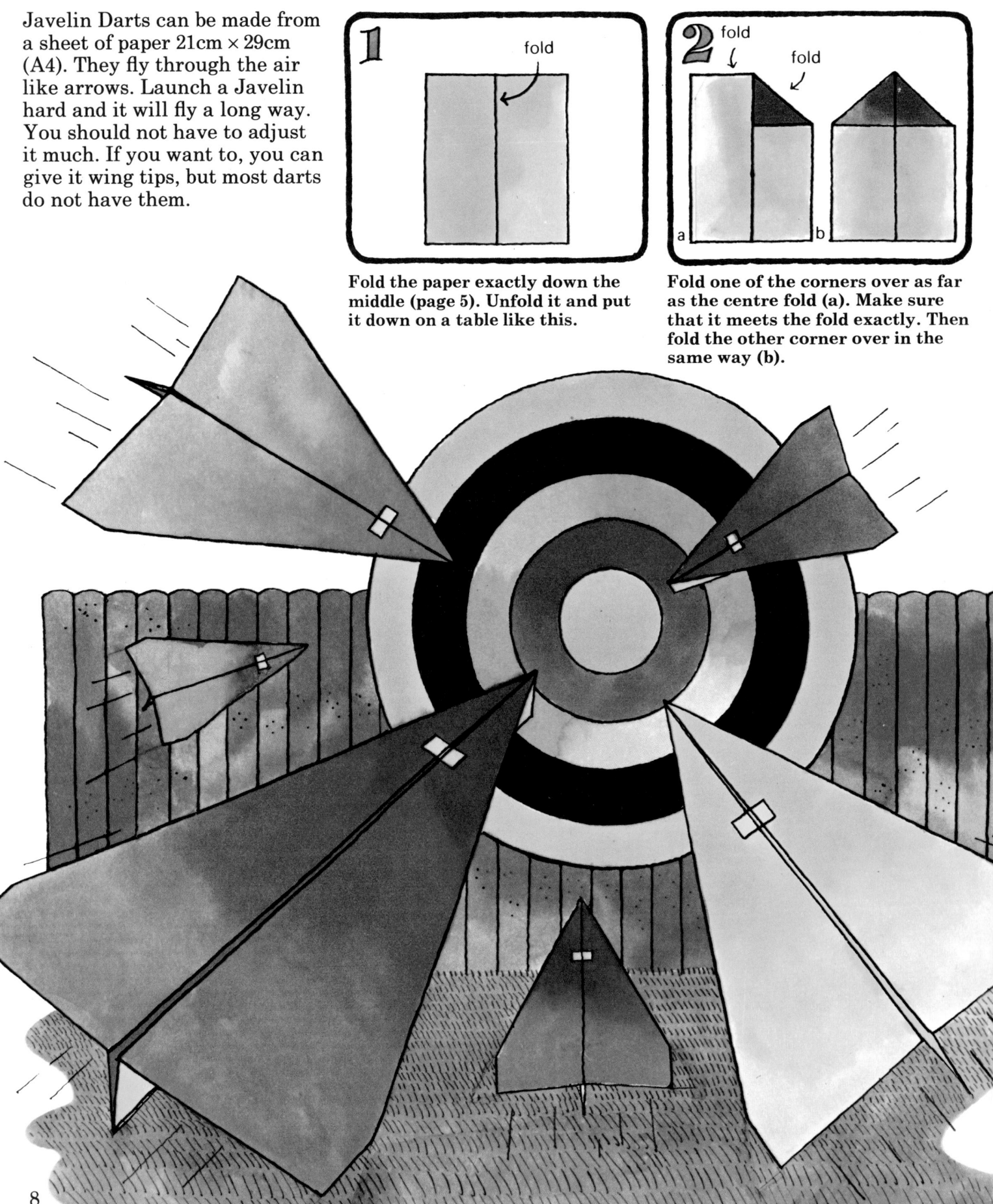

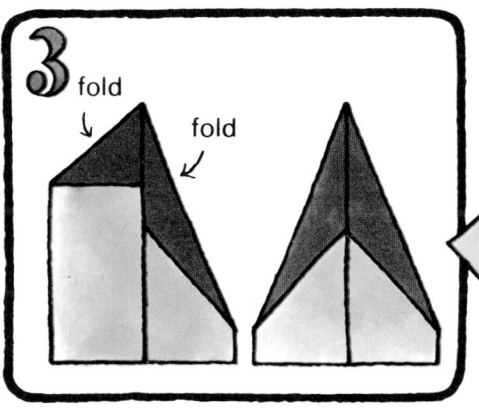

3 fold / fold

Fold the corners over again so that they meet at the centre fold.

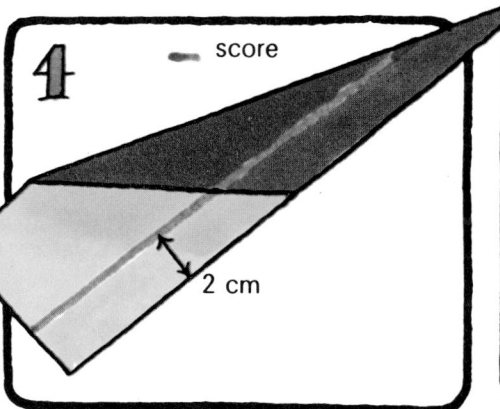

4 score / 2 cm

Fold the paper along the centre fold. Score a line about 2 cm from this fold all the way along.

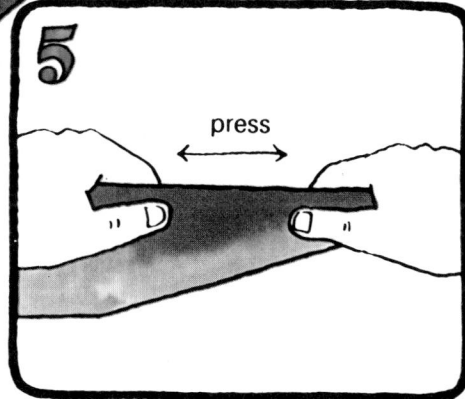

5 press

Fold the top wing down over the score line. Then fold the other wing down over the score line in the other direction. Press hard along the folds as shown.

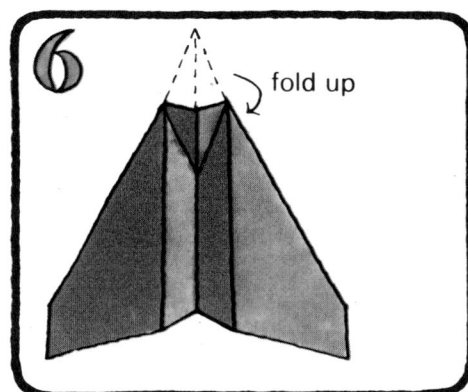

6 fold up

Open out the dart. Fold the pointed nose up on to the dart where the score lines end.

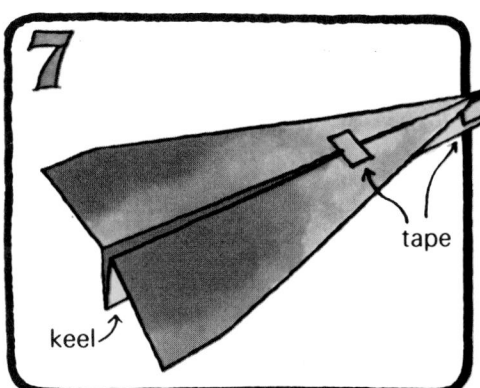

7 tape / keel

The paper under the wings is called a keel. Hold the dart by its keel like this. Put tape over the nose and on top of the wings.

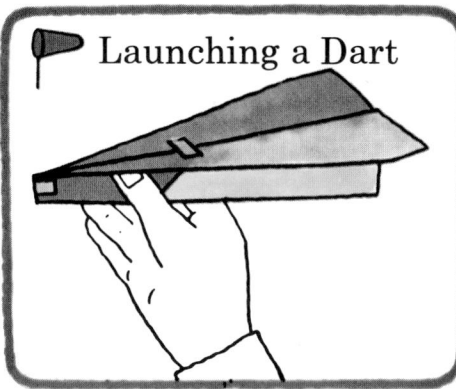

Launching a Dart

Point the dart down a little and throw it hard.

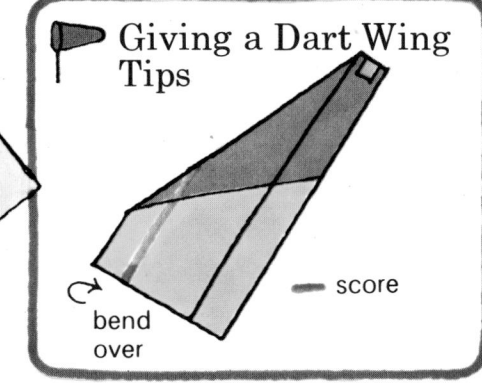

Giving a Dart Wing Tips

score / bend over

If you want to you can give the dart wing tips by folding the dart and scoring a line as shown. Open the dart out and bend the wing tips up a little.

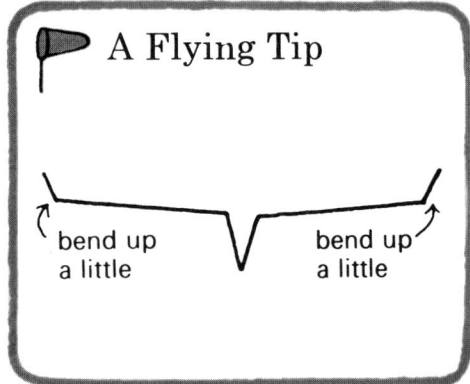

A Flying Tip

bend up a little / bend up a little

If you give the dart wing tips, hold the dart up in front of you and make sure that the wing tips are not too upright. You only need to bend them up a little.

Making a Long Fold

If the fold you want to make is longer than your ruler, fold the paper over the ruler, then slide the ruler along the groove and fold the rest of the paper over it.

Buffalo Mark 1 and 2

Buffalo Mk 1 and 2, with their big, heavy folded noses are very good at flying tricks. You can make them from a sheet of paper 21cm × 29cm. Ask for A4 paper. As they do not have keels like Javelin Darts, you will have to launch them in the same way that you launched the Free Flyer. (See page 7.)

Buffalo Mark 1

1 Buffalo Mk 1

mark on both edges

— score

Fold the paper in half and put it along the line at the top of this page like this. Mark A on both edges of the paper and score a line as shown.

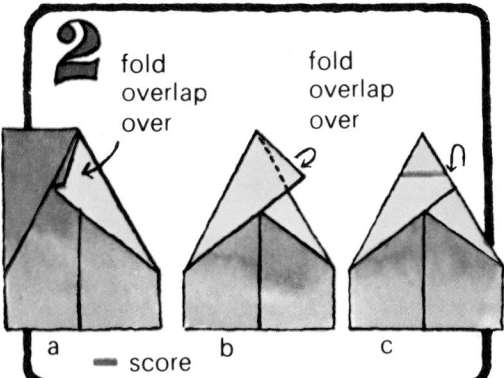

2

fold overlap over

fold overlap over

a   b   c

— score

Open the paper. Fold one corner along the score line (a), fold the other corner over and fold back any paper that overlaps (b). Score across the top and fold it back (c).

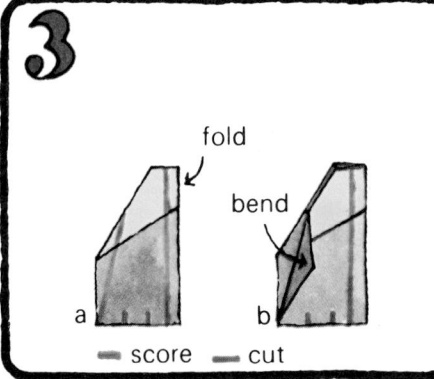

3

fold

bend

a   b

— score   — cut

Fold the paper in half like this. Score two more lines as shown (a). Bend the paper over both score lines and cut two snips in the bottom as shown (b).

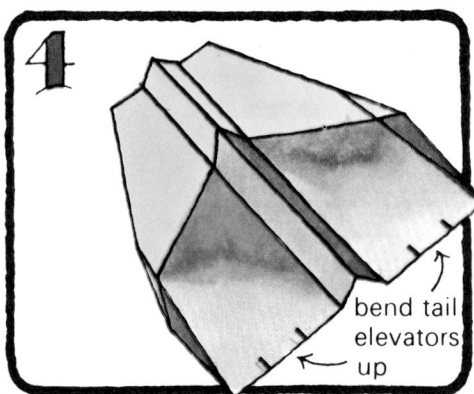

4

bend tail elevators up

Open the paper out again so that it looks like this. You launch it this way up. Bend the tail elevators up if it dives or glides too steeply.

Buffalo Mark 2

1 Buffalo Mk 2

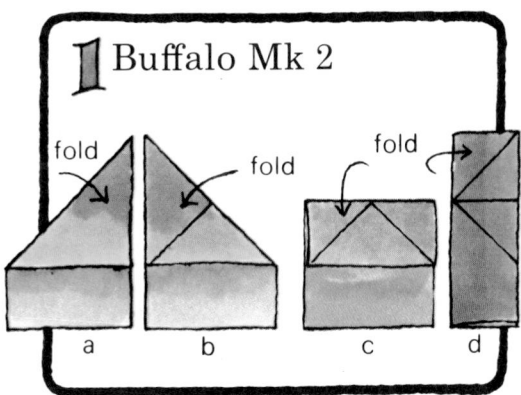

To make guide lines you will have to fold the paper four times, a, b, c, d, and unfold it four times. You unfold it after you have made each fold before you make the next.

2

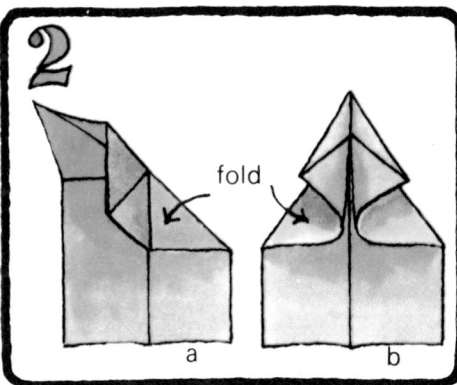

Open the paper out flat. Fold one side down like this (a). Then fold the other side down in the same way (b).

3

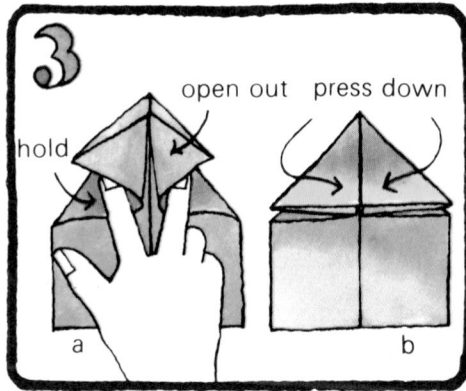

Hold the folds you have just made down with one hand. Open the top of the paper out with the other (a). Press the paper down as shown (b).

4

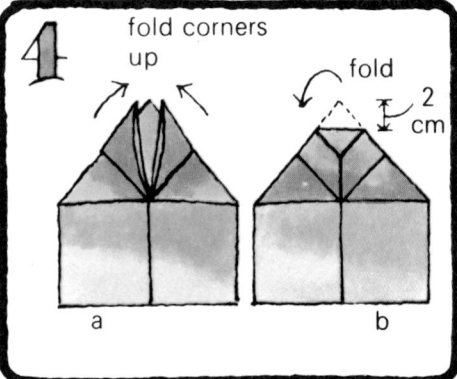

Fold the two corners up to the point (a). Press them down. Fold 2 cm of the pointed nose down on to the dart as shown (b).

5

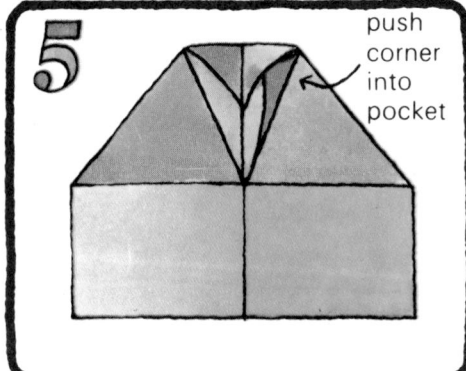

You will have made two pockets at the top of the paper. Push the remaining two corners into the pockets as shown.

6

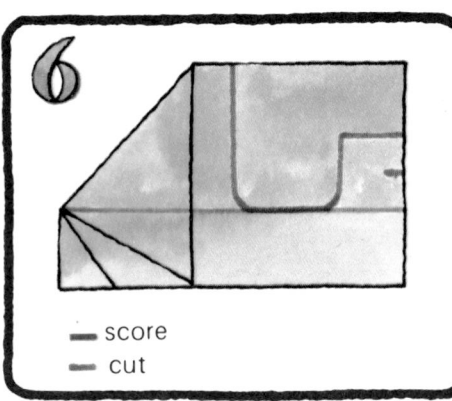

score
cut

Fold the paper in half and score a line as shown. Draw and cut out the aeroplane shape. Cut two tail elevator snips in the back.

7

Bend the paper over at the score line so that the plane looks like this. The middle should point downwards as shown. The dart is quite open. It has no keel.

The Air Scorpion

The Air Scorpion is a racing plane. It has swept-back wings and it flies very fast and straight.

You will need
THE PATTERN FOR ITS TAIL
  FIN ON PAGE 42
a sheet of paper 21cm × 29cm
a ball point pen for scoring
scissors
a ruler
sticky tape

B

Fold the paper in half like this. Put it along the line at the top of this page. Mark A and B on both edges of the paper.

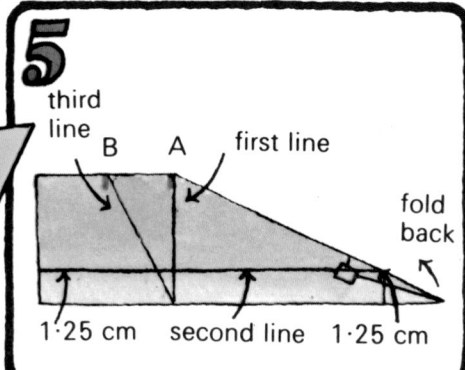

Fold the paper down the middle and fold the nose in. Draw three lines, one from A down to the fold, another across the bottom of the paper and the last from B as shown.

Launching it

Hold the plane by its keel. Point it down a bit and let it go gently.

The Air Scorpion

12

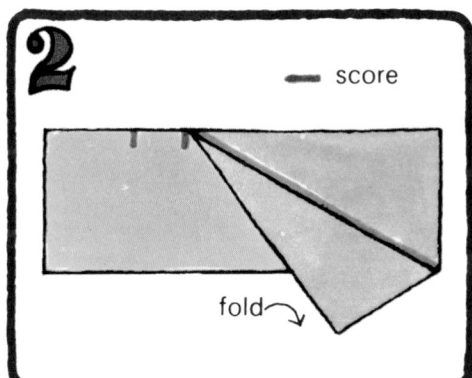

2 — score
fold

Score a line from A to the top of the fold. Fold one of the corners over along this line as shown. Then fold the other corner back the other way.

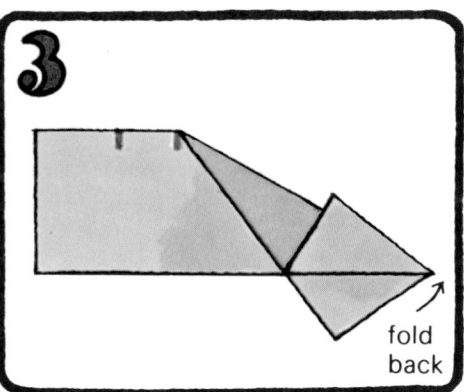

3
fold back

Fold both the corners back as shown.

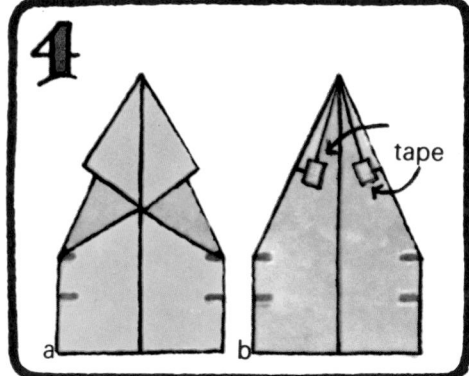

4
tape
a   b

Open the paper out. It should look like this from the front (a). Turn it over and fold both the corners over tightly. Tape them down (b).

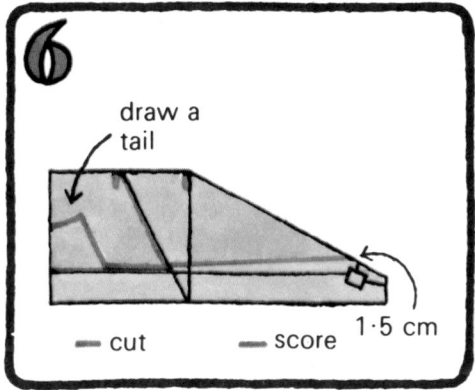

6
draw a tail
cut — score — 1·5 cm

Draw a tail shape and cut the plane out as shown. Score a line across the wings as shown. Score another across the tail.

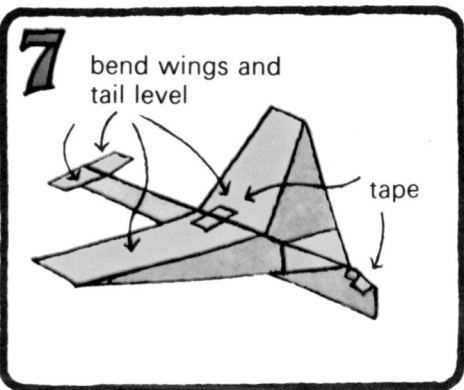

7
bend wings and tail level
tape

Bend the tail and wings along the score line so that they are level. Keep the wings in place with tape and tape the front of the nose.

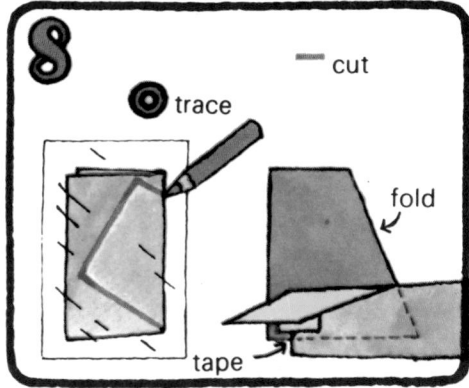

8 — cut
trace
fold
tape

Trace the tail fin pattern on to a folded piece of paper. Cut it out. Tape it inside the body of the plane, fold first, so that it sticks out a bit like this.

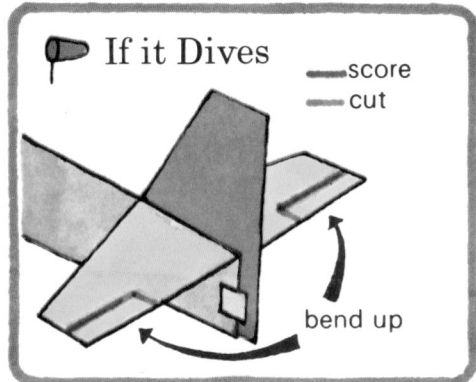

If it Dives — score — cut
bend up

You can stop it diving by giving it tail elevators. Make a cut each side of the tail fin as shown. Bend the tail elevators up a little. (See page 7.)

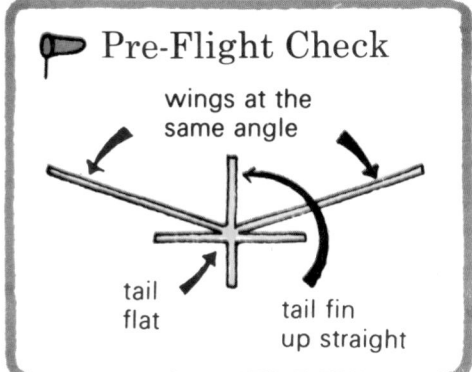

Pre-Flight Check
wings at the same angle
tail flat
tail fin up straight

Hold your plane up and see if it looks like this. The wings must be at the same angle. The tail should be flat and the tail fin should point straight up.

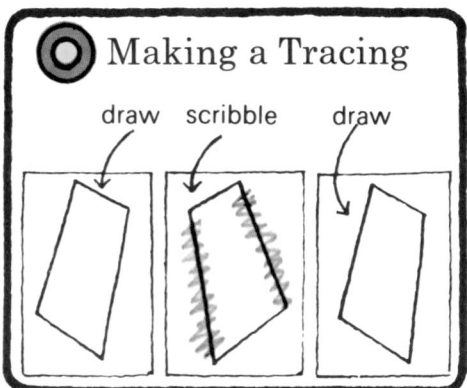

Making a Tracing
draw   scribble   draw

Draw the outline on tracing paper. Turn it over and scribble over the outline with a pencil. Put the tracing, right side up, on paper and draw round the outline again.

The Range Moth

You will need
THE PATTERN FROM
 PAGE 42
a big sheet of paper at least
 30cm × 44cm
tracing paper and a pencil
a ball point pen cap, bits of
 card or plasticine
scissors, sticky tape and glue
see page 13 on making a tracing

If you want to, you can make a
parachute as well.
You will need
some polythene 20cm × 20cm
a big paper clip
scissors and thread

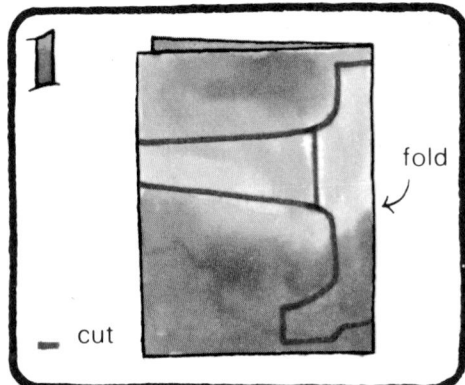

Trace the pattern on to a folded
piece of paper. Remember to trace
the score line as well. Cut the
plane out, but do not cut along
the fold.

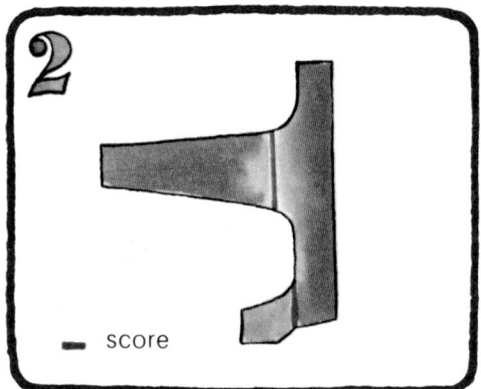

Put a ruler exactly on to the score
lines. Score one line across the
wing, score another line across the
tail as shown.

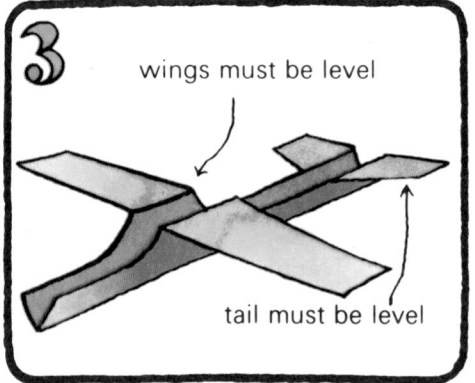

Bend the wings and tail down along
the score lines as shown.

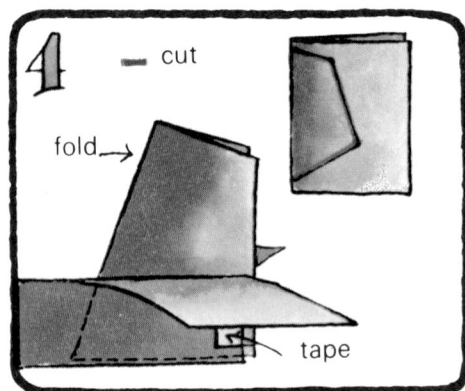

Trace the tail fin on to a folded
piece of paper. Cut it out, but not
along the fold. Tape the tail fin,
fold first into the inside back of the
plane as shown.

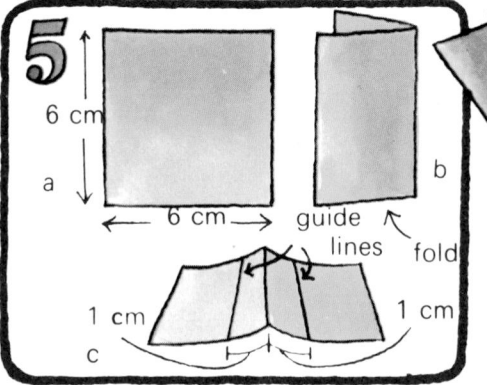

Cut out a piece of paper 6 cm ×
6 cm (a). Fold it in half (b). Open it
out and draw two guide lines 1 cm
from the fold as shown (c).

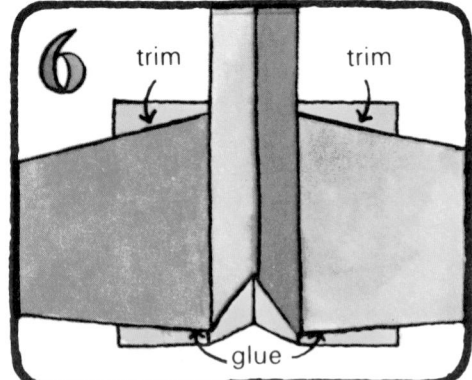

Glue the plane down on to this
piece of paper as shown. The wings
are following the guide lines you
drew on the piece of paper. Trim
any paper that overlaps.

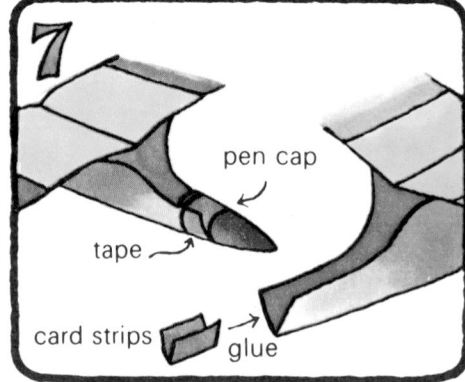

Tape the plastic cap of a felt or
ball point pen into the nose. If
you want to, you can cut out small
strips of card and glue them into
the nose instead.

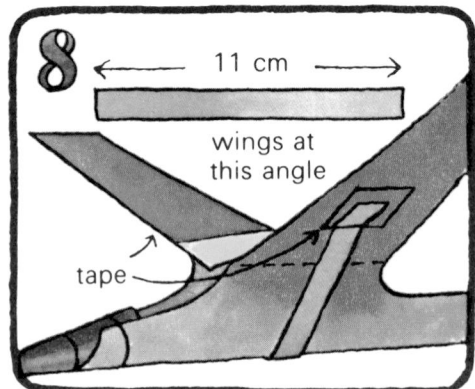

Cut out a narrow strip of paper
11 cm long. Fold it in half. Hold it
under the plane. Tape it to each
side of the wings so that the wings
tilt up at the same angle.

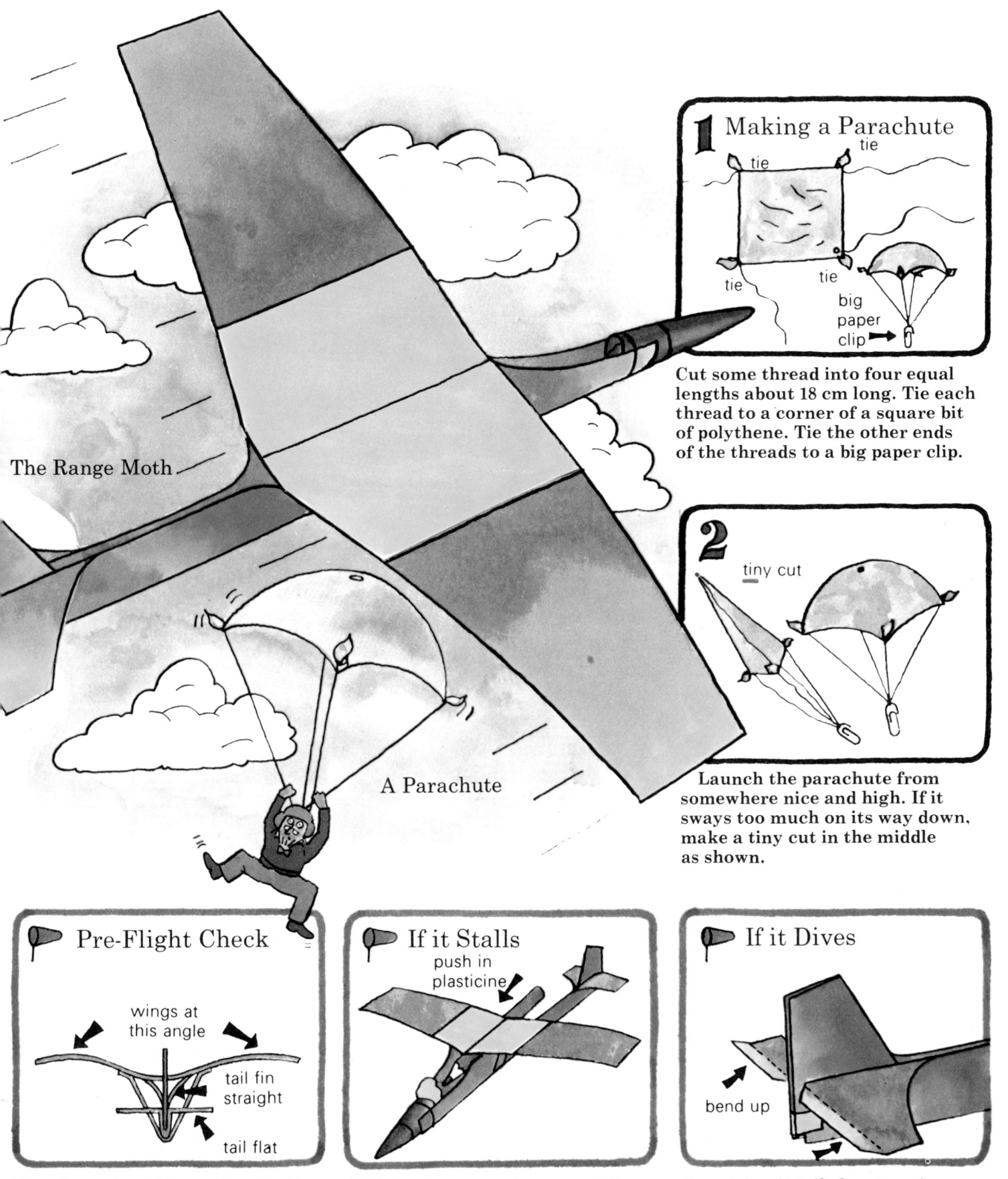

The Range Moth

A Parachute

1 Making a Parachute

tie
tie
tie
tie

big paper clip ➡

Cut some thread into four equal lengths about 18 cm long. Tie each thread to a corner of a square bit of polythene. Tie the other ends of the threads to a big paper clip.

2

tiny cut

Launch the parachute from somewhere nice and high. If it sways too much on its way down, make a tiny cut in the middle as shown.

Pre-Flight Check

wings at this angle

tail fin straight

tail flat

The plane should look like this if you hold it up in front of you. The tail fin must point straight up with the tail pieces flat. Wings must be at an angle.

If it Stalls

push in plasticine

Weight the top of the nose with plasticine until the plane glides smoothly. Then push the same plasticine into the pen cap with a pencil as shown.

If it Dives

bend up

Try giving it tail elevators (see page 7) and bend them up as shown.

The Moon Bug

You will find that the Moon Bug is a very easy aeroplane to make. See page 13 on making a tracing.

You will need
THE MOON BUG PATTERN
  FROM PAGE 42
a sheet of paper 21cm × 29cm
tracing paper and a pencil
scissors and sticky tape
a ruler
a ball point pen for scoring

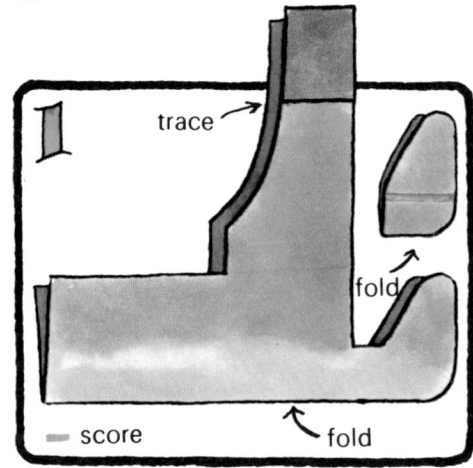

Fold the paper and trace the plane and tail pattern on to it. Cut it out, but do not cut along the fold. Trace the lines on the wings and tail. Score the tail as shown.

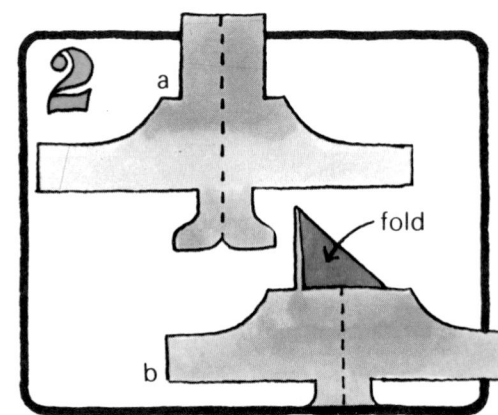

To make the nose of this aeroplane, you will have to make guide lines. Start with the paper opened out (a). Then, fold one of the corners over as shown (b).

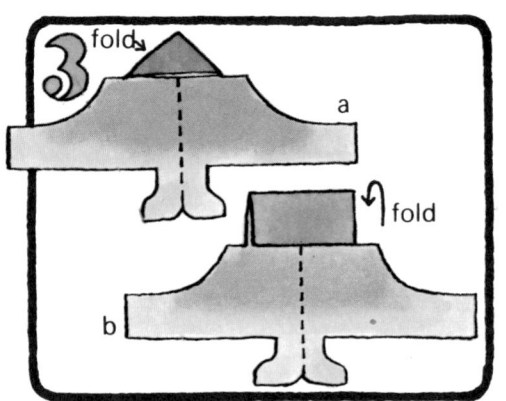

Fold the other corner over (a). Open the paper out and make a third fold (b) like this. Open the paper out for the last time and you have your guide lines.

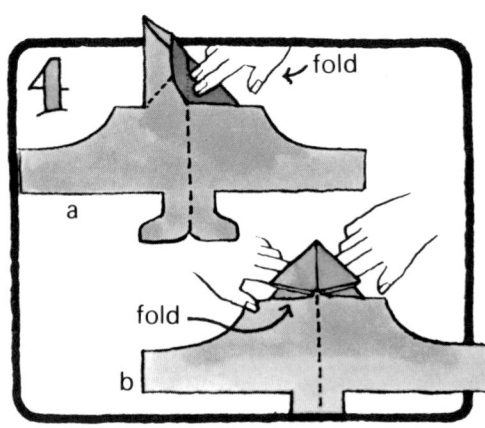

Make a fold like this on one side of the paper (a). Hold this fold down and fold the other side down in the same way (b).

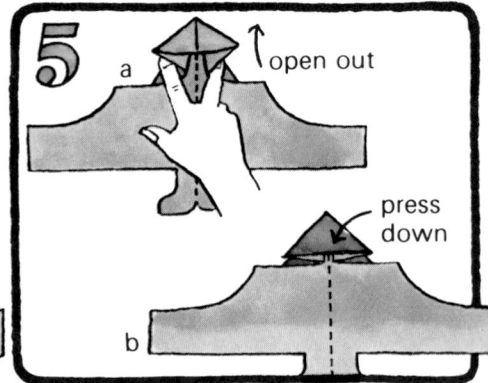

Hold the paper folds in place with one hand and with the other open the paper above them out (a). Then press all the paper down (b).

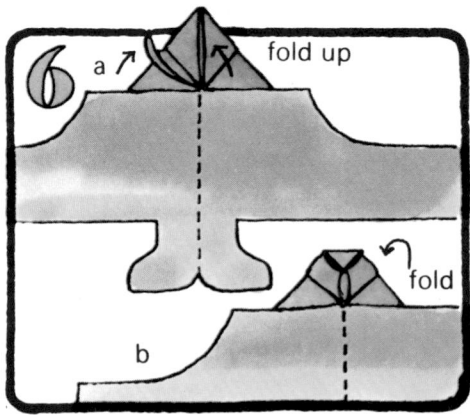

Fold the two bottom corners up as shown (a). Then fold the pointed end down (b).

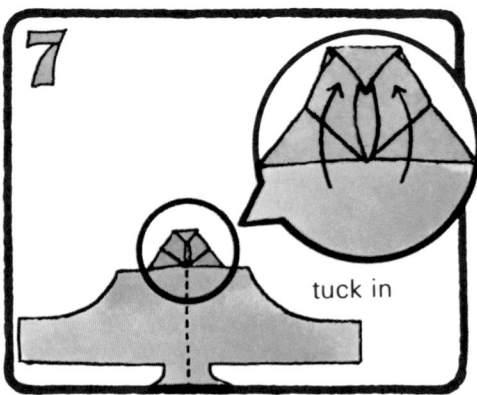

When you folded the pointed end down, you made little pockets at the top of the paper. Tuck the two free corners right into the pockets as shown.

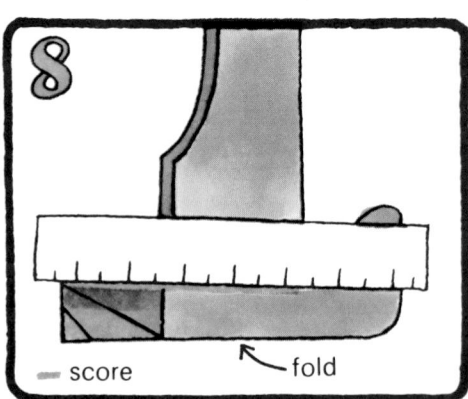

Fold the paper in half. Put your ruler along the top of the fuselage and score a line across the wings.

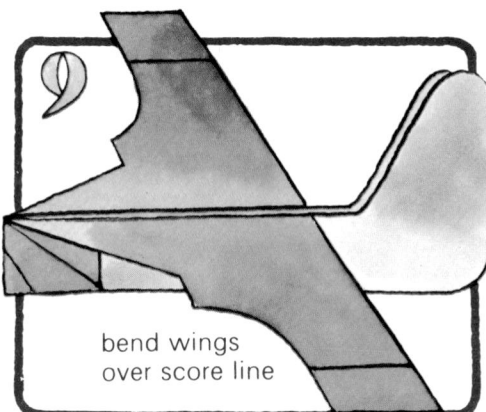

Bend the wings back along the score line so that they are level.

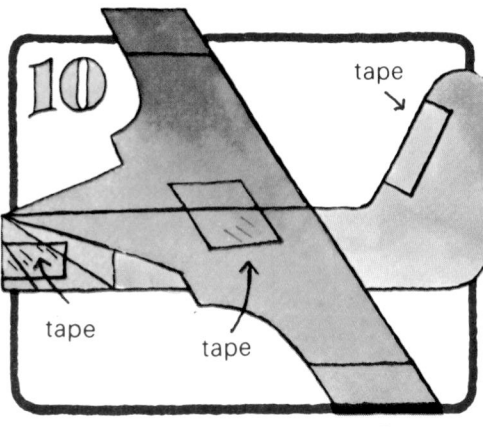

Tape the plane together at the nose and across the top of the wings. Tape the tail fin together as shown.

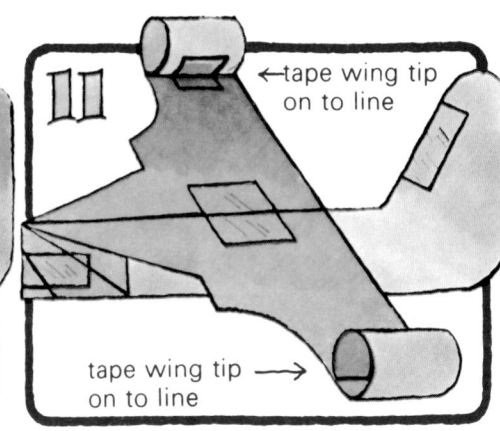

Curl the wing tips over and tape them on to the wings at the traced lines as shown.

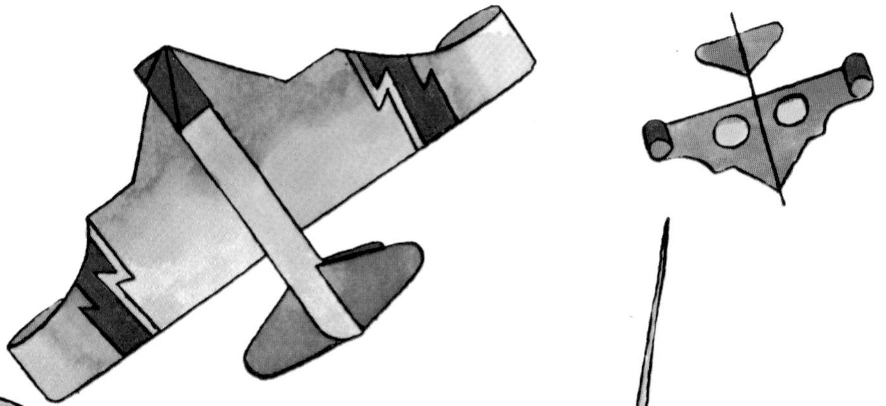

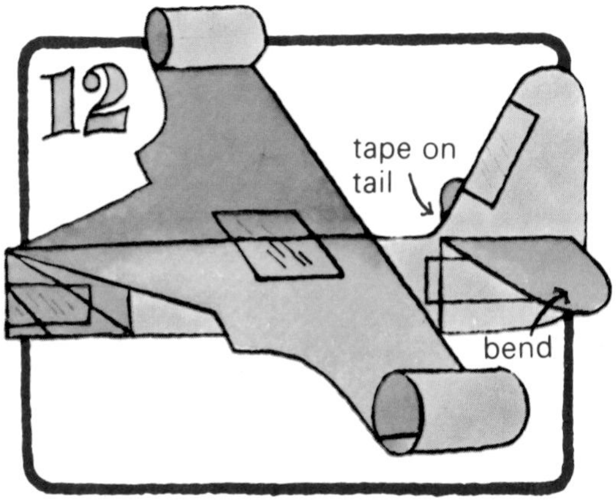

12

tape on tail

bend

Bend the tail along its score lines and tape it under the tail fin so that the back of the plane looks like this.

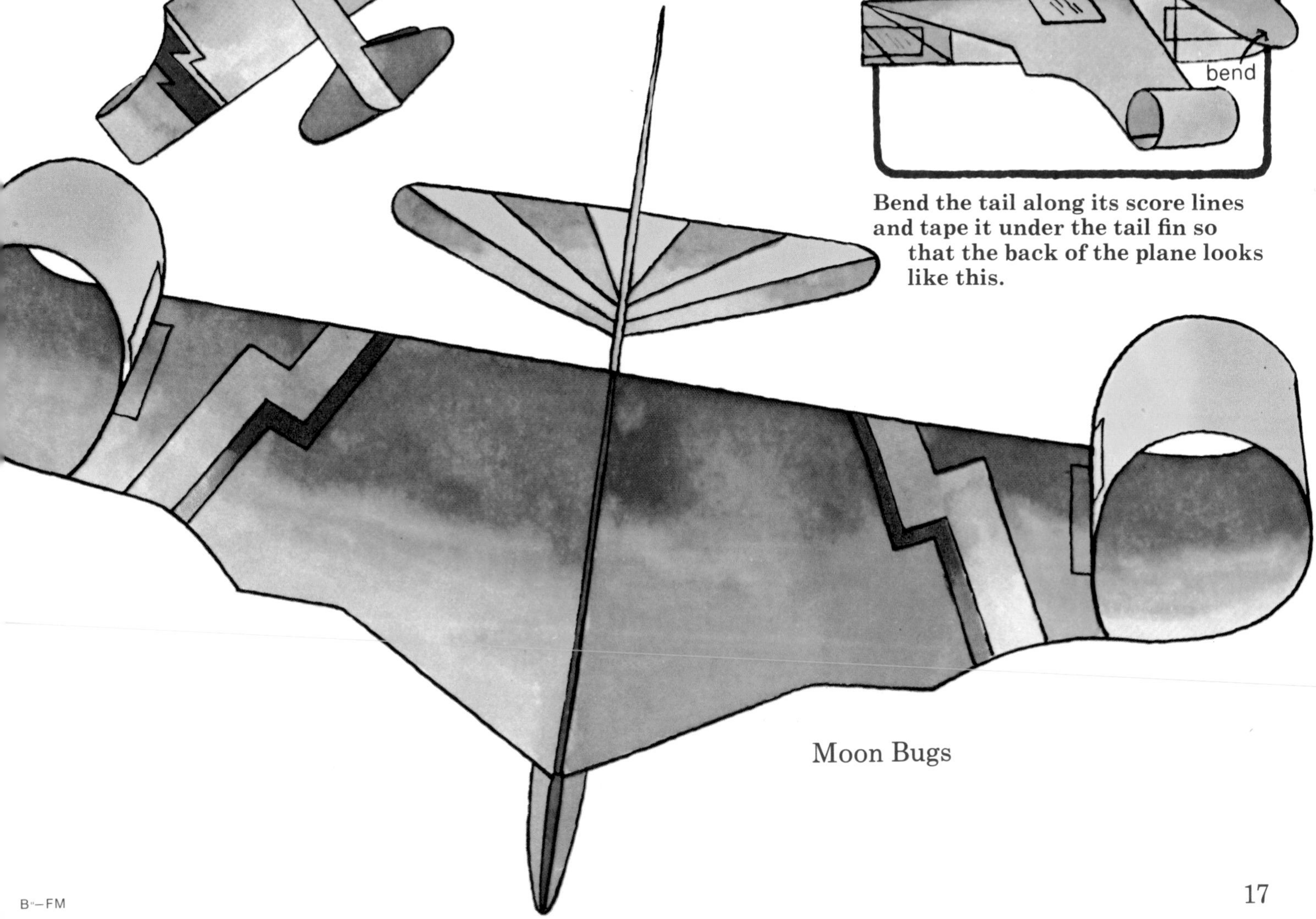

Moon Bugs

The Drinking Straw Glider

The Drinking Straw Glider has a special kind of curved wing. It is called a cambered wing. The camber gives the plane a little more lift. See page 13 on making a tracing.

You will need
THE PATTERN FROM
    PAGE 43
a sheet of paper for the wings and tail
card from a document folder
2 drinking straws
tracing paper and a pencil
scissors and a ruler
plasticine or silver foil
strong glue and sticky tape

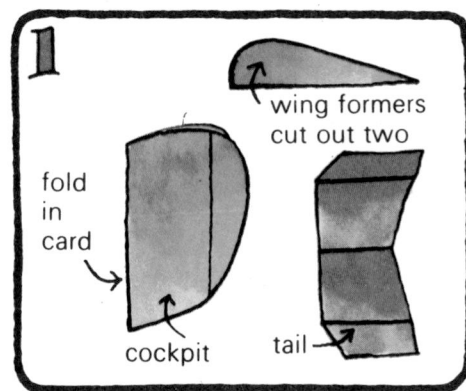

Trace and cut out a card cockpit, two card wing formers and a paper tail. Remember to trace all the lines on the patterns.

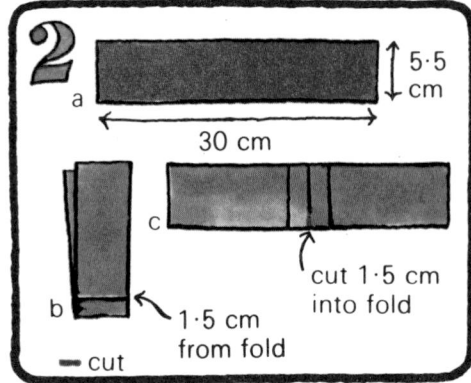

Cut out a paper wing as shown (a). Fold the paper in half and draw a line 1·5 cm from the fold (b). Open the wings out and cut a notch into the fold as shown (c).

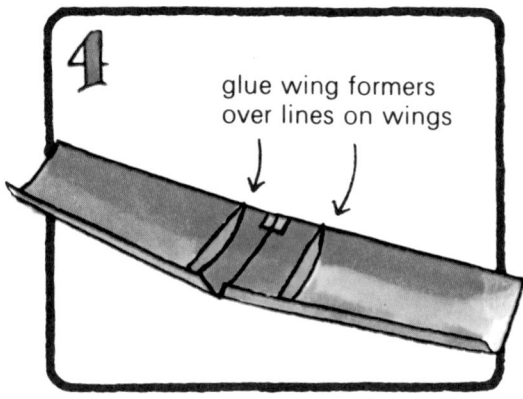

Put glue on the curved edge of the wing formers. Glue them on to the wings along the lines you drew each side of the notch.

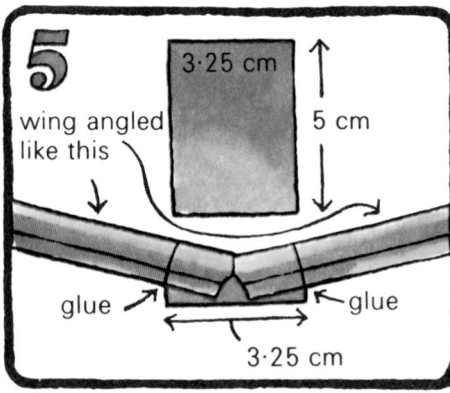

Cut out a piece of card 5 cm × 3·25 cm. Glue its long edges to the bottom edges of the wing formers so that the wings become angled like this.

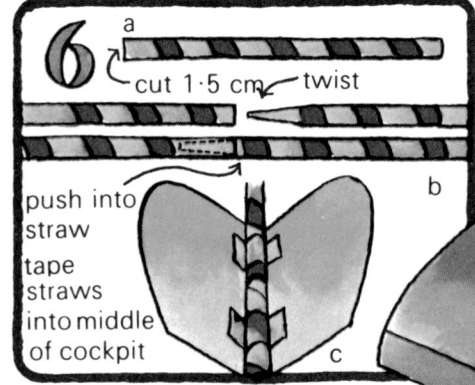

Slit the end of a straw (a). Twist the slit end into a point, push it into another straw to make one long straw (b). Tape the middle of this long straw into the cockpit (c).

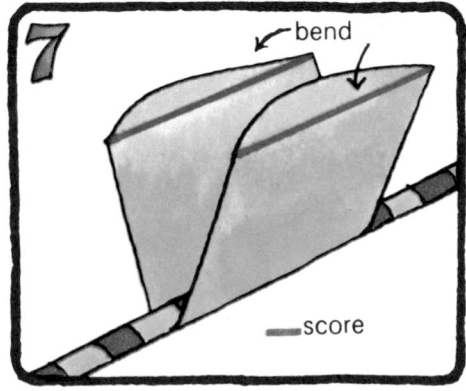

Score the cockpit along the lines you traced. Bend the cockpit along the score lines as shown.

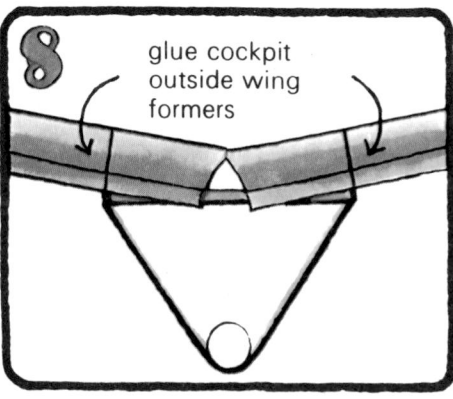

Glue together the wings and cockpit with the cockpit outside the wing formers as shown.

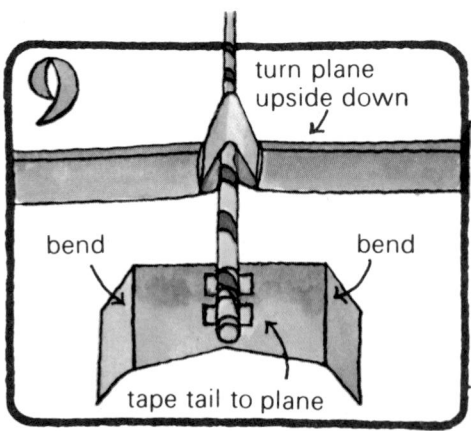

Put the plane upside down and tape the tail on to it like this with the straw lying along the line down the middle of the tail. Bend the sides of the tail as shown.

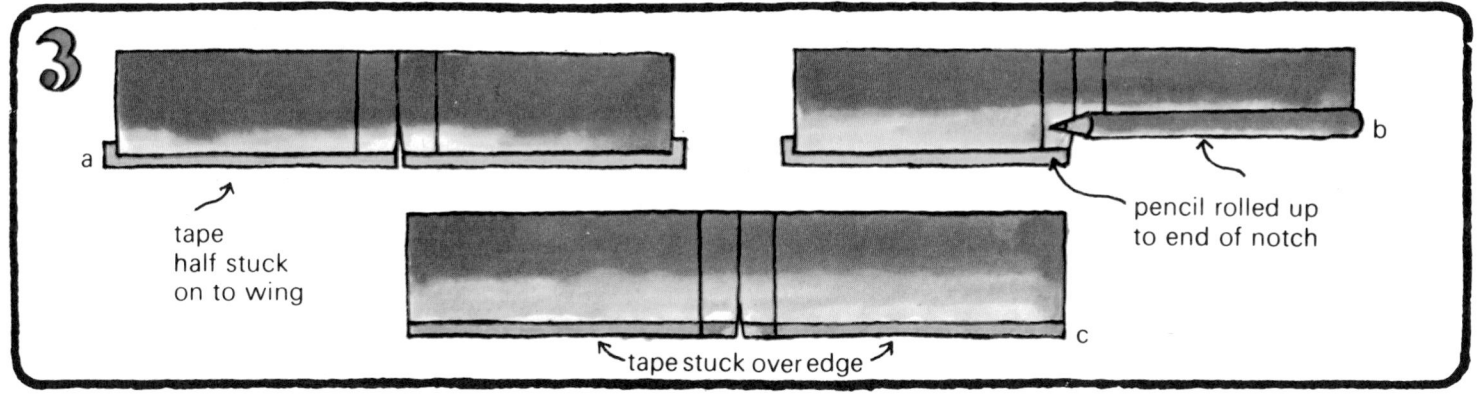

3

a tape half stuck on to wing

pencil rolled up to end of notch b

tape stuck over edge c

Half stick some tape along the notched edge of one wing as shown (a). Then put a ROUND pencil on to the unstuck half of the tape in line with the front wing edge.

Roll the pencil up the wing as far as the end of the notch (b). Then unroll the pencil and take the tape off it very carefully. Do it again on the other wing.

Fold the free edge of the tape up over the wing edge like this (c). The curve you have just made is called a camber.

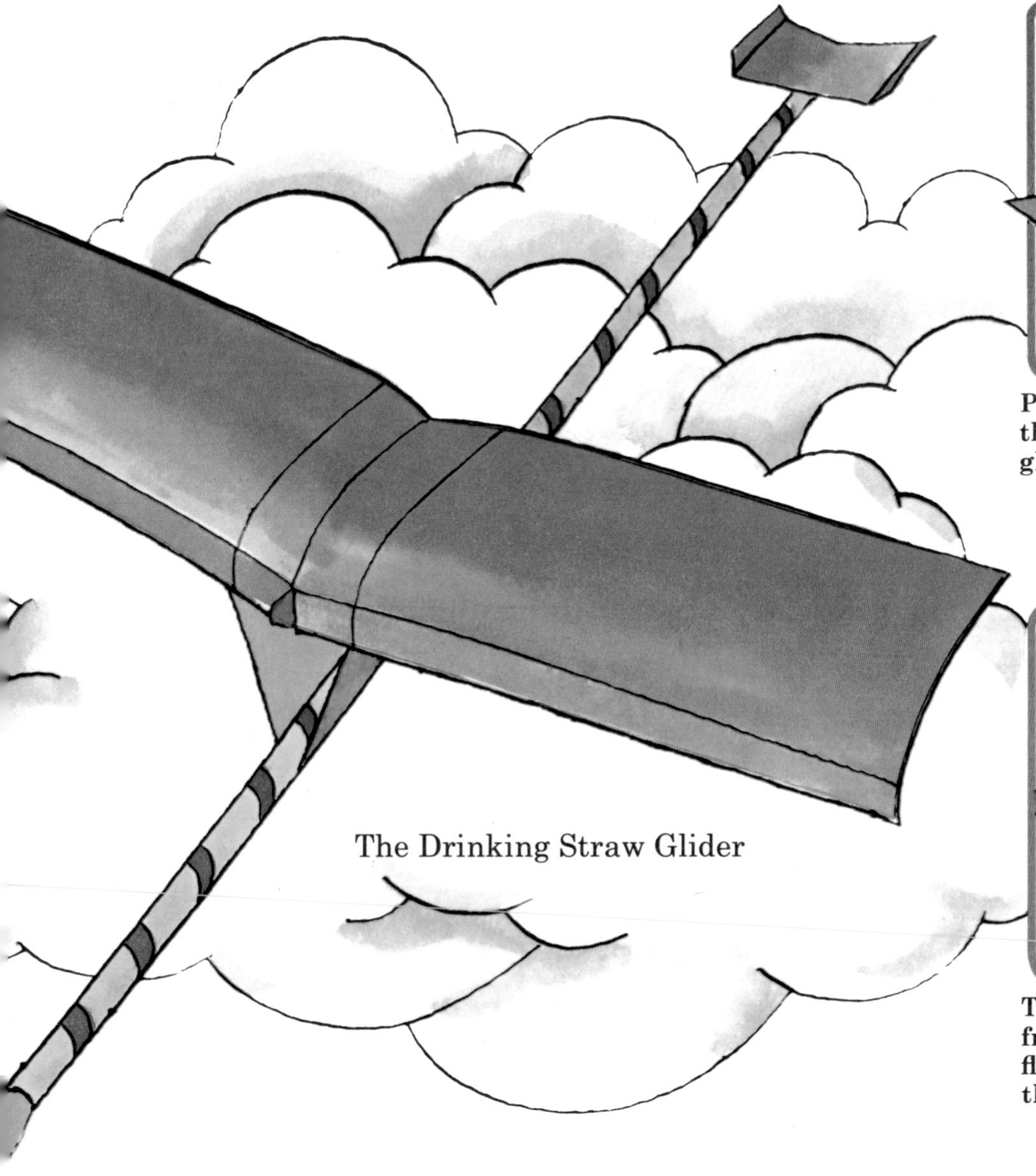

silver-foil or plasticine

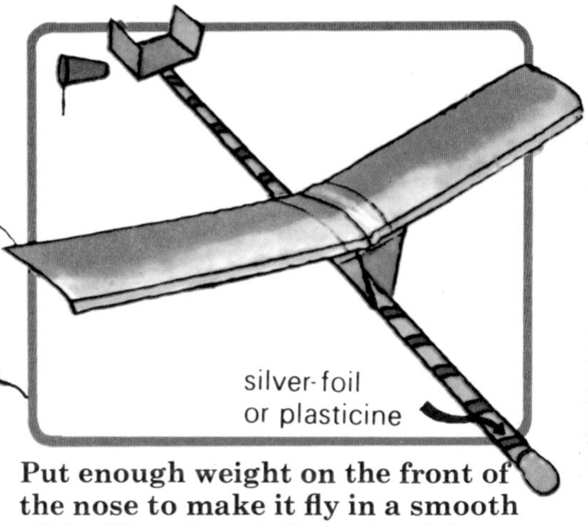

Put enough weight on the front of the nose to make it fly in a smooth glide. Use silver foil or plasticine.

The Drinking Straw Glider

Pre-Flight Check

wings at same angle

tail flat

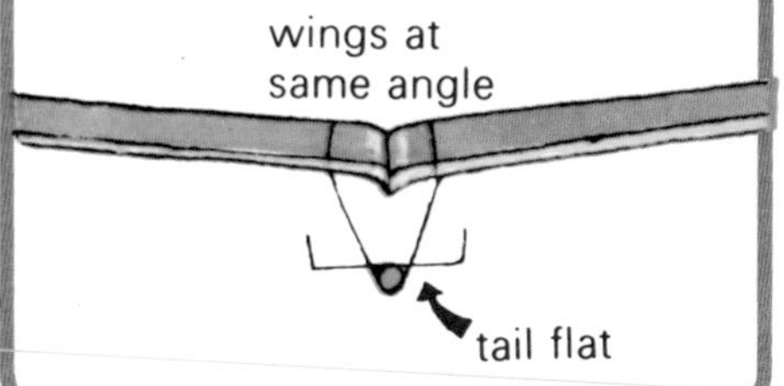

The Glider should look like this from the front. The tail must be flat and the wings must be at the same angle.

Jungle Fighter KH20

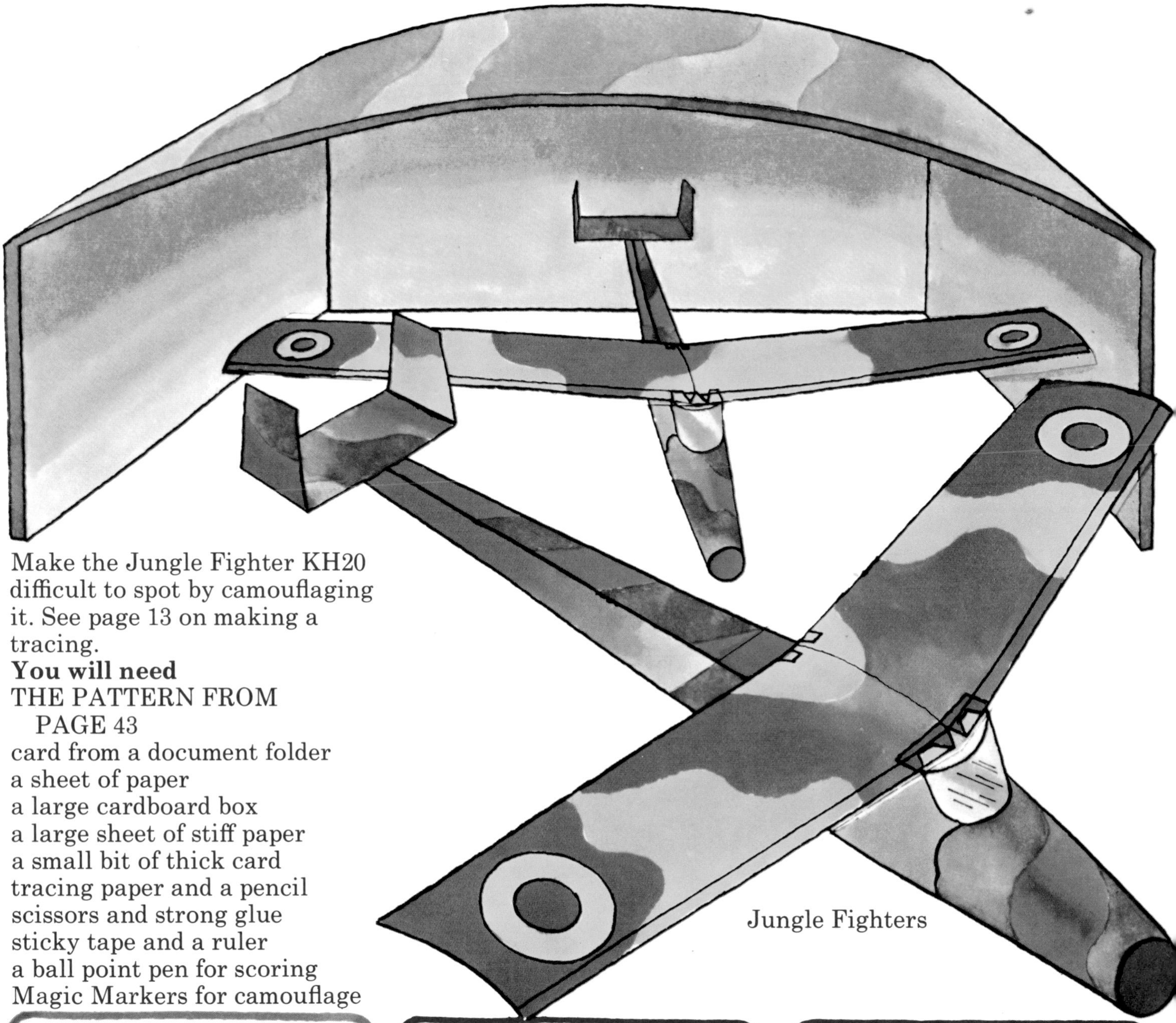

Make the Jungle Fighter KH20 difficult to spot by camouflaging it. See page 13 on making a tracing.

You will need
THE PATTERN FROM
   PAGE 43
card from a document folder
a sheet of paper
a large cardboard box
a large sheet of stiff paper
a small bit of thick card
tracing paper and a pencil
scissors and strong glue
sticky tape and a ruler
a ball point pen for scoring
Magic Markers for camouflage

Jungle Fighters

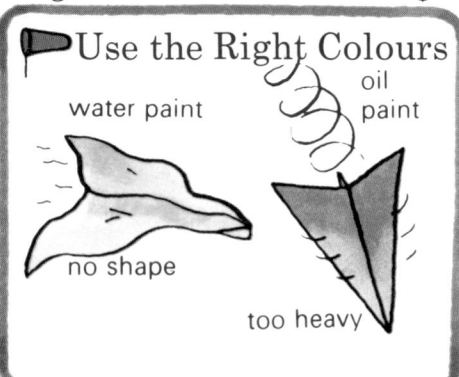

Use the Right Colours

water paint

no shape

oil paint

too heavy

Do not use water-based paints on the planes. The paper will crumple up and lose its shape. Oil paints are too heavy. Colour them with Magic Markers.

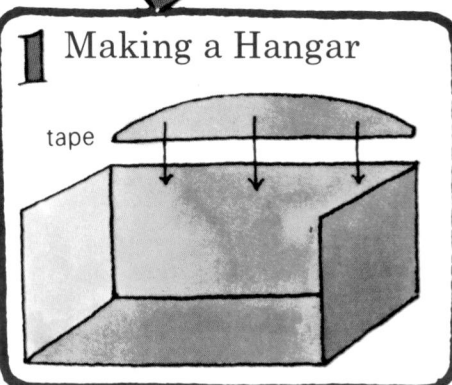

1 Making a Hangar

tape

Put a large cardboard box on its side. Cut off the top side. Cut out a curved shape from the extra cardboard as shown. Tape the shape on to the back of the box.

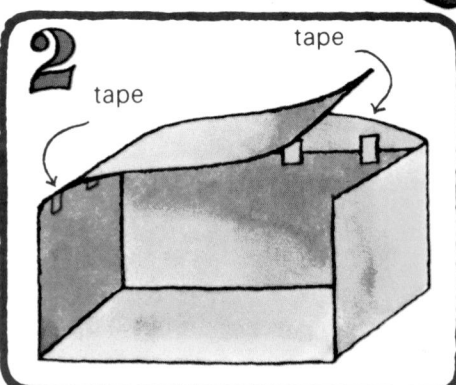

2

tape

tape

Make a roof by laying some stiff paper over the curved shape and taping it to the sides of the box. Camouflage it by painting it the same colour as its surroundings.

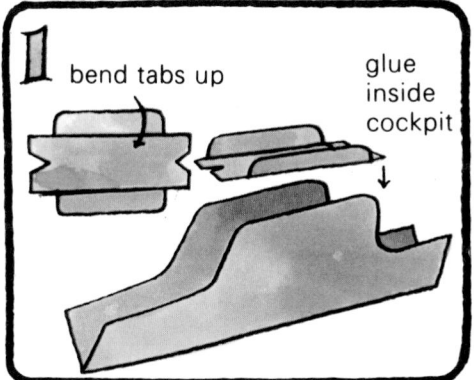

1 bend tabs up · glue inside cockpit

Trace and cut out a card cockpit and cockpit top. Score and bend the cockpit top as shown and glue it into the top of the cockpit.

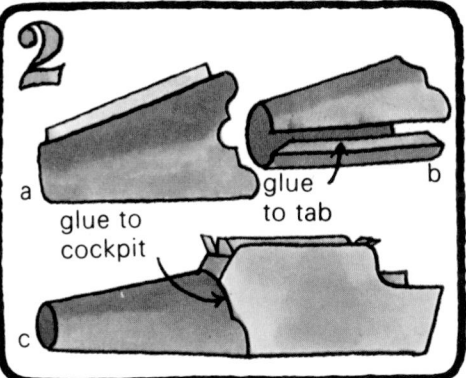

2 a · glue to cockpit · glue to tab · b · c

Trace and cut out a paper nose (a). Bend the nose piece round, dab glue on its tab and join it up (b). Glue it to the front of the cockpit (c).

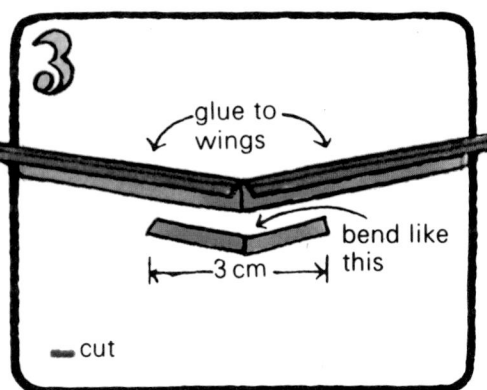

3 glue to wings · 3 cm · bend like this · cut

Trace and cut out its paper wings. Make a small snip as shown and camber them (page 18). Cut out a narrow strip of thick card. Bend it, glue the wings on to it as shown.

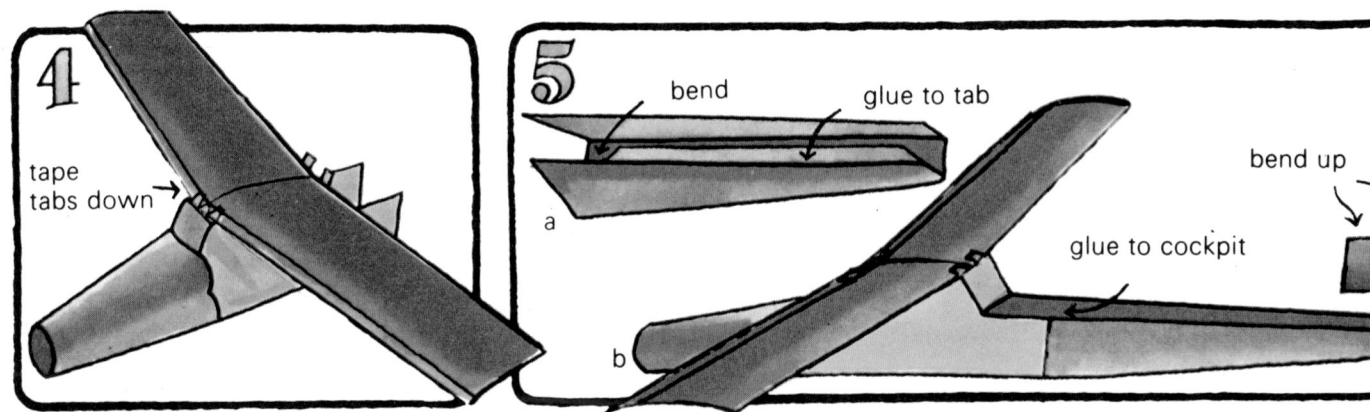

4 tape tabs down

Put the wings on top of the cockpit. Bend the front and back cockpit top tabs over the wings and tape as shown.

5 bend · glue to tab · bend up · a · b · glue to cockpit · glue

Trace and cut out a paper fuselage. Bend it as shown. Put glue on its tab and glue it together (a). Trace and cut out a paper tail. Bend the tail sides up where shown.

Glue the fuselage into the back of the cockpit like this. Glue the tail on top of the end of the fuselage as shown (b).

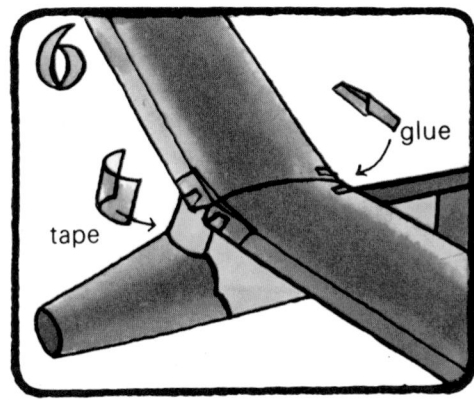

6 glue · tape

Put a strip of sticky tape over the front of the cockpit. Trace and cut out a card cockpit back. Score it and glue it into the back of the cockpit.

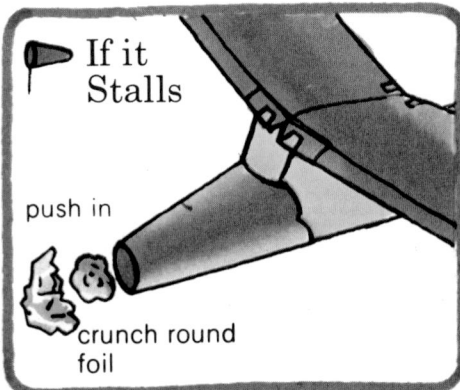

If it Stalls · push in · crunch round foil

If it stalls it means that the nose is not heavy enough. Make the nose heavier by squeezing plasticine into it or crunching silver foil around it.

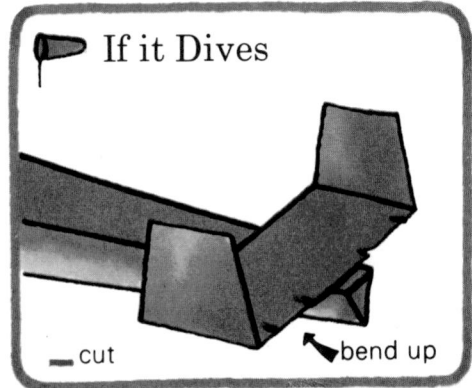

If it Dives · cut · bend up

If it dives, it means that the nose is too heavy. Take some weight off the nose or make tail elevators (page 7), bend them up as shown.

The Hawkeye Devastator

The Hawkeye Devastator flies out of doors. Launch it against the wind. Its propeller spins round when it flies. See page 13 on making a tracing

You will need
THE PATTERN ON PAGES 44 and 45
card from a document folder
a big sheet of paper
tracing paper and a pencil
a rubber band and a straw
a 3cm long big-headed pin
2 ball point pens
scissors and a ruler
sticky tape and glue
a needle and thread

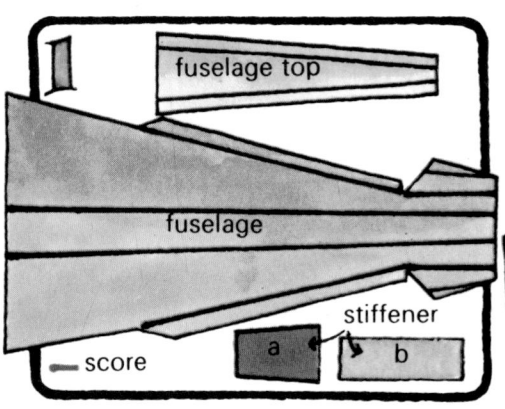

Trace and cut out a paper fuselage, a paper fuselage top and two card stiffeners. Score the fuselage as shown.

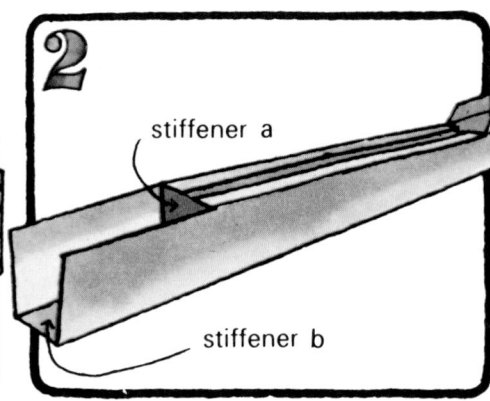

Bend the fuselage sides up along the score lines. Glue stiffener (a) and (b) into the fuselage as shown. Stiffener (b) should touch the bottom edge of stiffener (a).

The Hawkeye Devastator

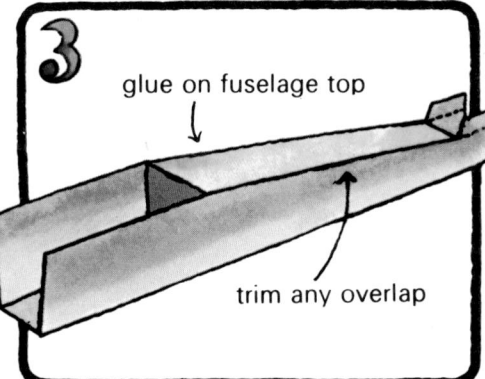

3 glue on fuselage top — trim any overlap

4 bend — score — bend

5 stiffener — fuselage and cockpit pieces level — glue on cockpit pieces

Bend the fuselage tabs in and glue the fuselage top on to the fuselage like this. When the glue is dry, trim off any overlapping paper.

Trace and cut out two card cockpit pieces. Score them both like this. Bend the bottom cockpit tabs up so that they lie flat on a table.

Glue the cockpit pieces on to the sides of the fuselage. Do this on a flat surface so that the bottom edge of each cockpit is in a straight line with the fuselage.

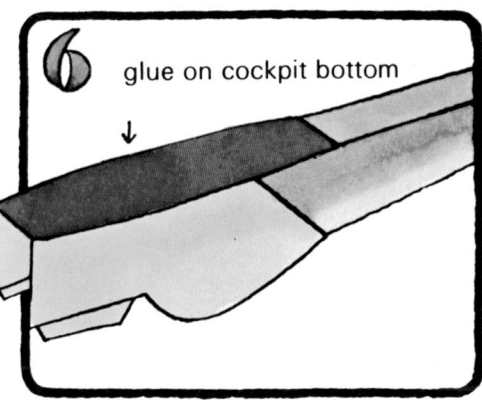

6 glue on cockpit bottom

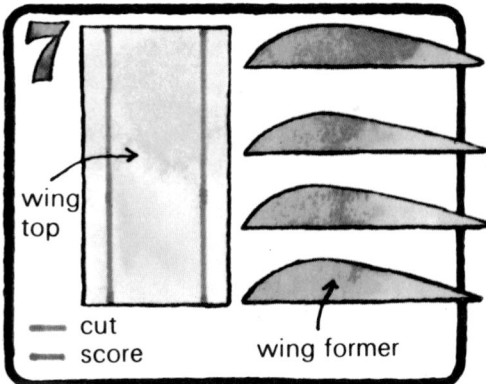

7 wing top — cut — score — wing former

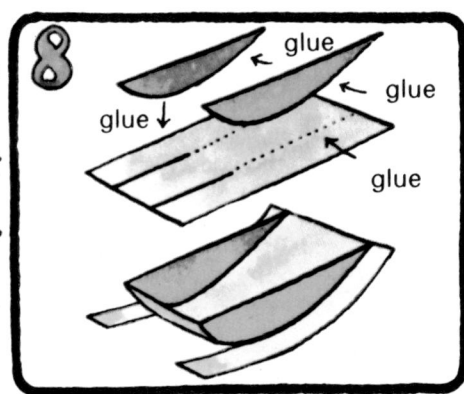

8 glue — glue — glue — glue

Trace and cut out a card cockpit bottom. Turn the fuselage over. Put glue on the tabs at the bottom of the cockpit and glue the cockpit bottom on as shown.

Trace and cut out a card wing top and four card wing formers. You must trace the score and cut lines on the wing top. Then score and cut it like this.

Put glue on to the curved edges of two of the wing formers. Glue them to the wing top along the score and partly cut lines as shown.

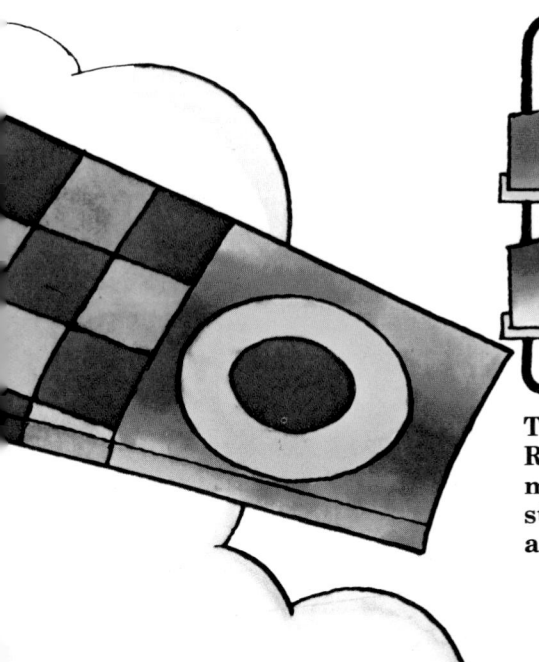

9 underside of wings — wing strut mark — tape — wing strut mark

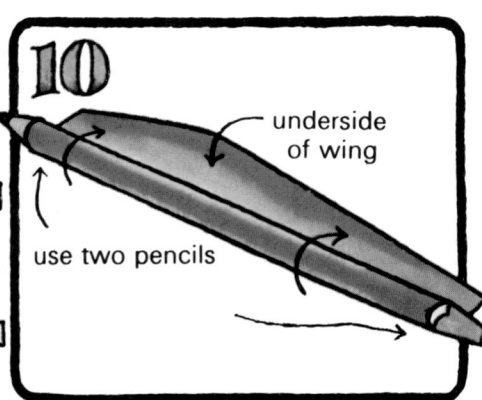

10 underside of wing — use two pencils

Trace and cut out two card wings. Remember to trace the wing strut marks. Put sticky tape on the straight edge of each wing as shown.

Camber each wing (page 19). You will have to use TWO round pencils instead of one. Make sure that they touch each other. Roll them both forward at the same speed.

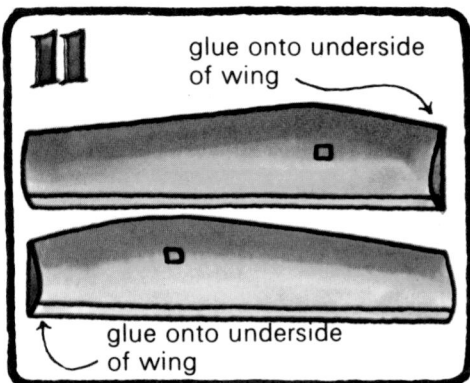

11 glue onto underside of wing

glue onto underside of wing

Put glue on to the curved edges of the other two wing formers and glue them on to the wings so that they look like this.

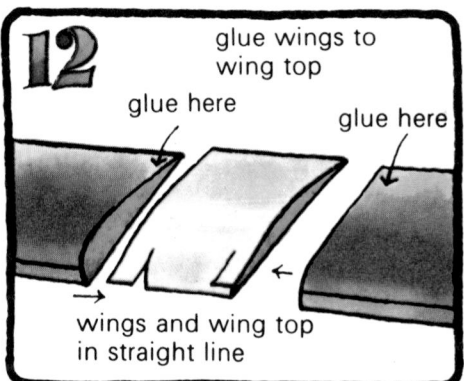

12 glue wings to wing top

glue here

glue here

wings and wing top in straight line

Glue the wing formered edges of the wings under the wing top flaps as shown. Make sure that the front edges of the wings and wing top lie in a straight line.

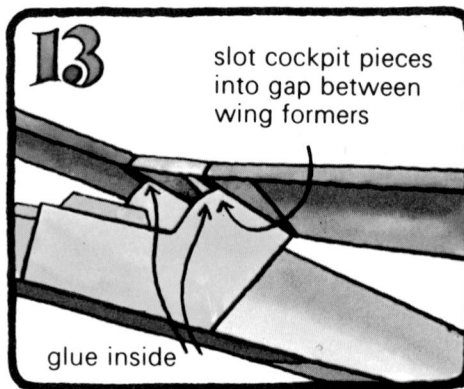

13 slot cockpit pieces into gap between wing formers

glue inside

Put glue on the inside of the curves at the top of the cockpit pieces and slip them up into the wing top so that each piece slots between two wing formers.

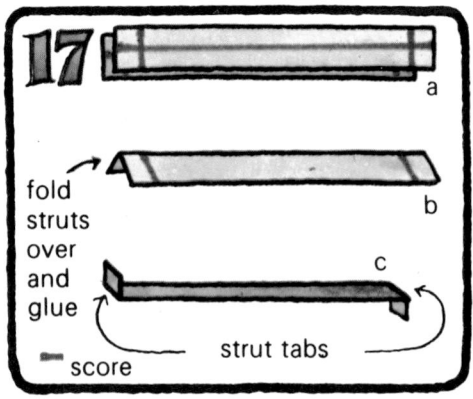

17 a

fold struts over and glue

b

c

score

strut tabs

Trace and cut out two card struts. Score each one as shown (a). Fold each one down the middle score line and glue (b). Bend along the other score lines as shown. (c).

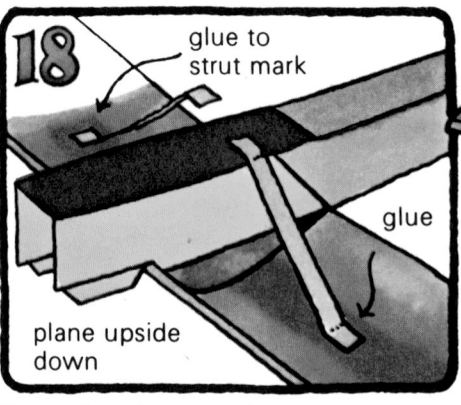

18 glue to strut mark

glue

plane upside down

Turn the plane upside down. Glue one of the strut tabs on to the wings over the wing strut mark. Do the same with the other strut on the other wing.

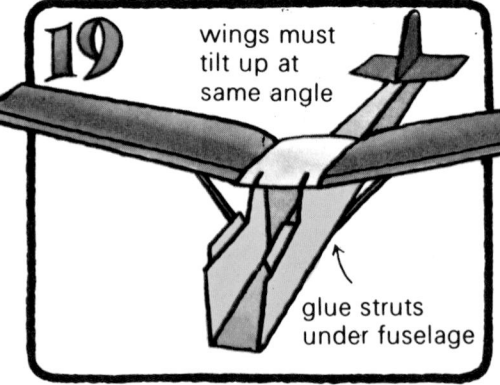

19 wings must tilt up at same angle

glue struts under fuselage

Turn the plane over. Move the free end of each strut tab up and down the fuselage base until both wings are at the same angle. Then glue the strut tabs on to the base.

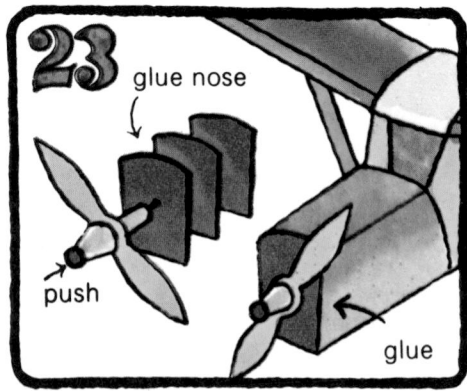

23 glue nose

push

glue

Trace and cut out three card noses. Glue them together. Push the long propeller pin firmly through them as shown. Glue them into the nose like this.

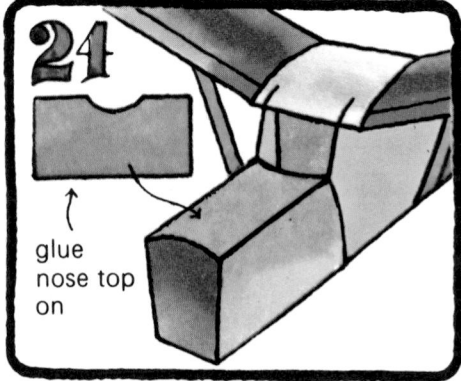

24 glue nose top on

Bend the tabs at the front of the cockpit pieces inwards. Trace and cut out a paper nose top. Glue it round the front of the cockpit.

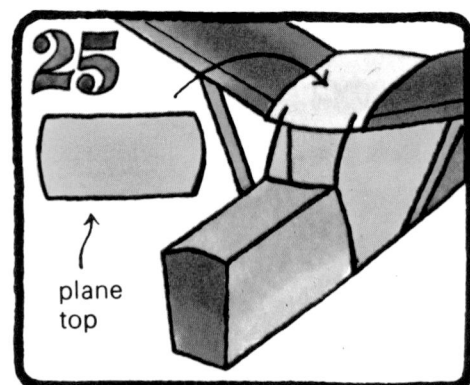

25 plane top

Trace and cut out a paper plane top. Put glue on to it and glue it over the middle of the wings so that it hides the score and cut marks on the wing top.

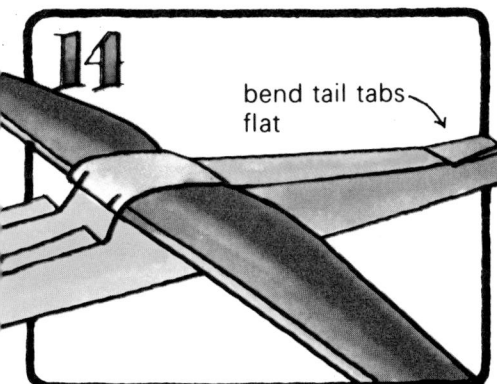

14

bend tail tabs flat

Bend the tail tabs at the end of the fuselage down on to each other so that they form a flat and level surface on which to glue the tail.

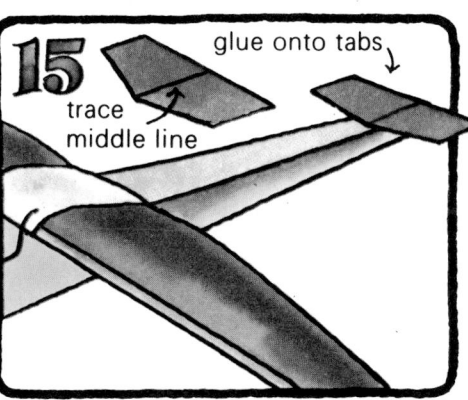

15

glue onto tabs

trace middle line

Trace the tail and the line going across it on to card. Cut it out. Put glue on the tail tabs and glue the tail on to them with the line going exactly down the middle.

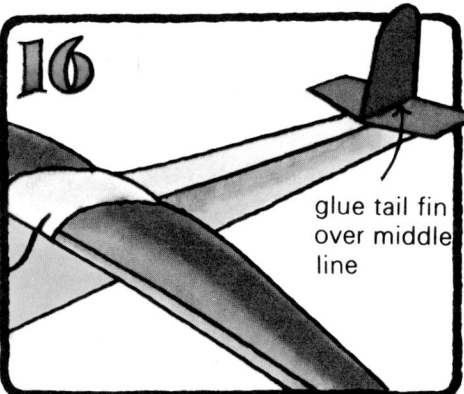

16

glue tail fin over middle line

Trace and cut out a card tail fin. Glue it down on to the middle line on the tail as shown.

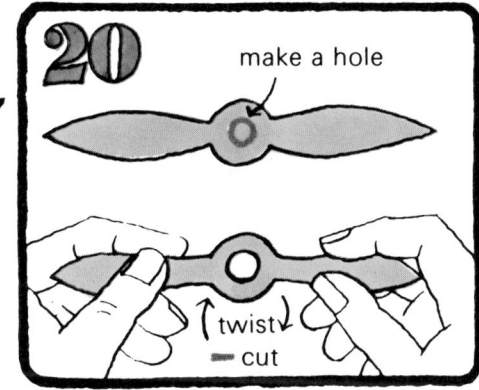

20

make a hole

twist

cut

Trace and cut out a card propeller. Make a hole with a knitting needle where shown. Gently twist one blade in one direction and the other in the other direction.

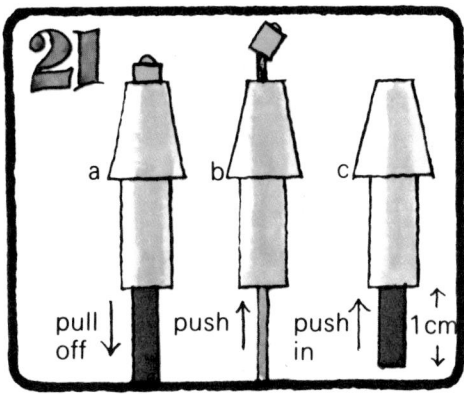

21

a b c

pull off

push in

push in

1 cm

Pull out the inside tube of a ball point pen (a). Push the ball point out of the bearing with a long pin (b). Cut 1 cm off the inside tube, push it back into the bearing (c).

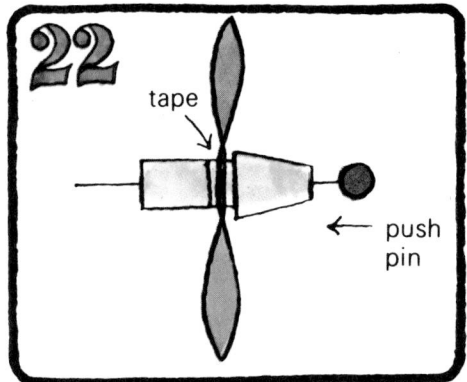

22

tape

push pin

Push the bearing through the hole in the propeller as shown. Tape the propeller to the bearing. Push the long big-headed pin through the hole in the middle of the bearing.

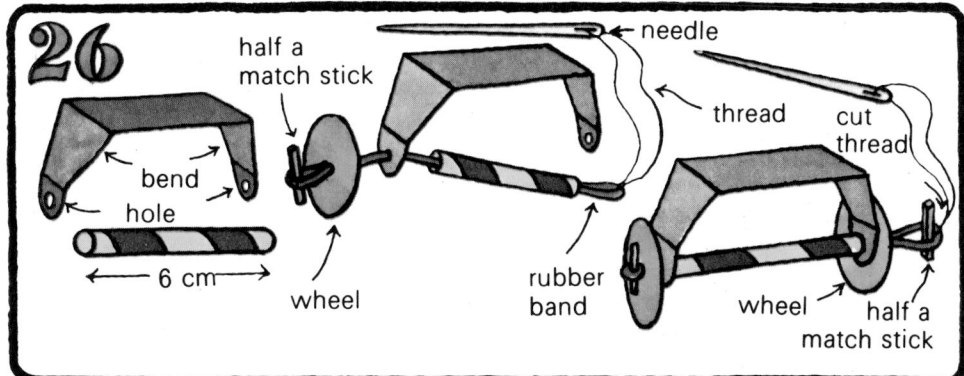

26

half a match stick

needle

thread

cut thread

bend

hole

6 cm

wheel

rubber band

wheel

half a match stick

Trace and cut out two card wheels and a card undercarriage. Make holes where shown. Score the undercarriage and bend its sides. Cut a straw as shown. Push a

needle, thread and rubber band through undercarriage, wheels and straw as shown. Stop the rubber band ends with half a match stick. Cut the thread.

27

glue to fuselage

Turn the plane upside down again. Glue the undercarriage on to the base of the cockpit just in front of the struts as shown.

Flying Tips

If you have managed to make your aeroplanes glide smoothly in a straight line, you might like to try making them fly in other ways. On this page you can find out how to make the different controls on an aeroplane that make it fly in different directions and perform flying tricks. Some of these, like looping-the-loop and S-bends take a lot of practice.

Making a Plane with a Keel turn left and right

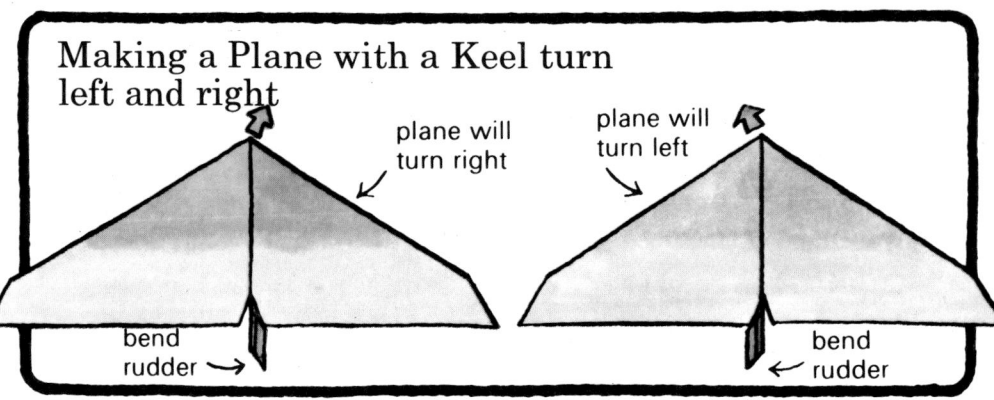

Planes with a keel like darts and Air Scorpions can be made to turn left and right by making a short snip through the keel just at the back under the wings and sticking the two sides together with tape. This is a rudder. Bend the rudder left to make the plane turn left, bend it right to make the plane turn right.

Making a Plane without a Keel turn left and right

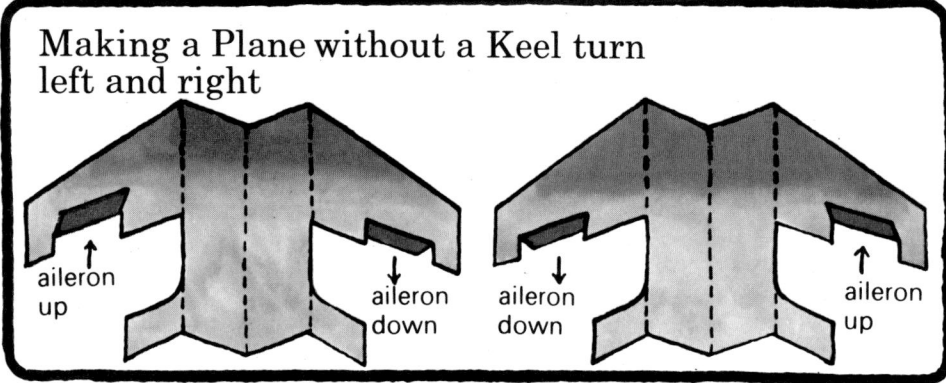

To make these planes turn you can give their wings ailerons. Make two cuts on each wing as shown. To make a plane fly to the left, bend the left aileron up and bend the right aileron down. To make a plane fly to the right, bend the right aileron up and the left one down.

Planes with Tail Fins

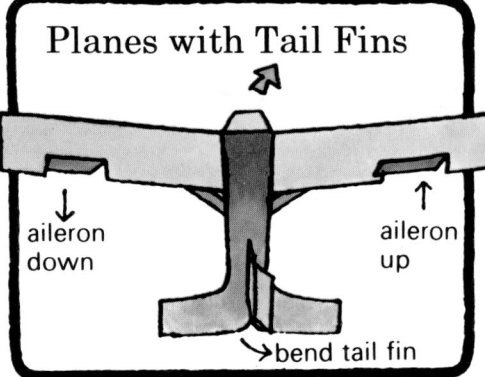

If your plane has ailerons and a tail fin, bend the ailerons in the usual way and bend the end of the tail fin to point in the direction you want the plane to fly.

Turning by Launching

A plane set to fly straight can be made to fly left by launching it at this angle. Tilt it in the other direction to make it turn right. This is launching it in a bank.

S-Bends

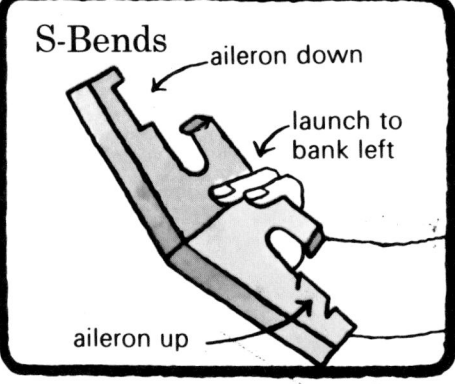

If you find it easy to launch your plane in a bank, try making it do an S-Bend. Set the controls to make it fly one way then launch it in a bank in the opposite direction.

Looping-the-Loop

Some people can make their planes loop-the-loop. Bend the tail elevators up, point the plane down and launch it very hard. This takes a lot of practice.

Flying out-of-Doors

tail elevators up

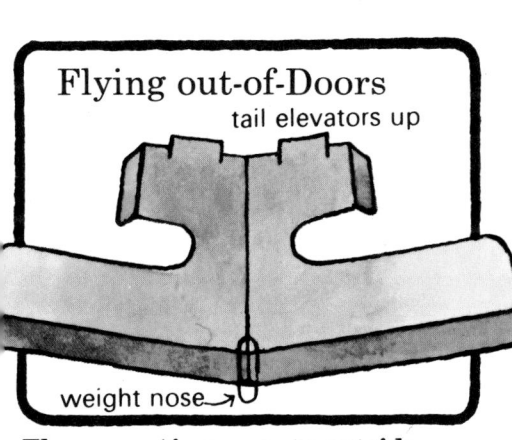

weight nose →

There are air currents outside which make it more difficult for a paper plane to fly. Try making your plane heavier by weighting the nose. Bend the elevators up.

1 Flying in a Wind

Aeroplanes can do strange things in a wind. If you launch a plane so that it flies in the same direction as the wind, it will fly much faster than it would inside.

2

If you launch a plane in the opposite direction to the way the wind is blowing, it may fly backwards like this.

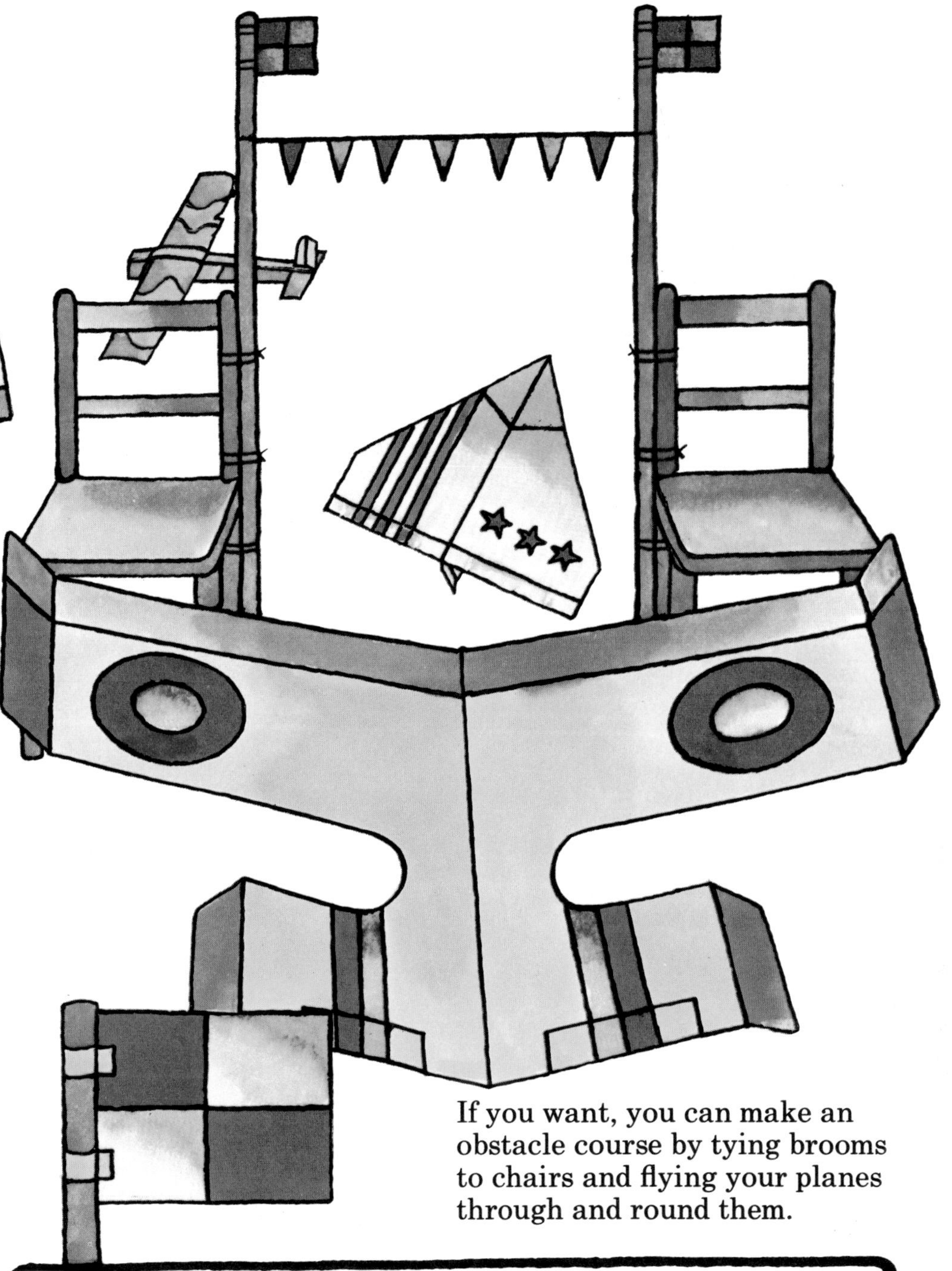

If you want, you can make an obstacle course by tying brooms to chairs and flying your planes through and round them.

Fling Gliding

Heavier planes can be exciting to fly by fling gliding. Tie one end of a piece of string to the edge of a wing, tie the other end to a strong stick or ruler. Bend the tail elevators up a bit. Hold the stick and turn round and round facing the stick all the time. See how long you can make the string without losing control.

Air Race

This is a game to test your skill at flying paper planes. Any number of players can play it. Everybody will need a paper plane and a counter. What you do is to make yourselves an aerobatics course like the one on page 27. You fly your plane on the course and then you move your counter along the board. The number of spaces you move your counter depends on how you fly your plane. Each flying trick is worth a different number of points. If you fly your plane to the left, it is worth 2 points, so you move your counter on 2 spaces on the board. Have a look at the score board and see what each trick is worth. Fly your planes in turn. When your counter lands on a space, you have to do what it says on the box. Try not to let your counter land on the hazard boxes. The player whose counter gets to the airport at the end of the course first is the winner. If you want, you can play the game with dice and counters only.

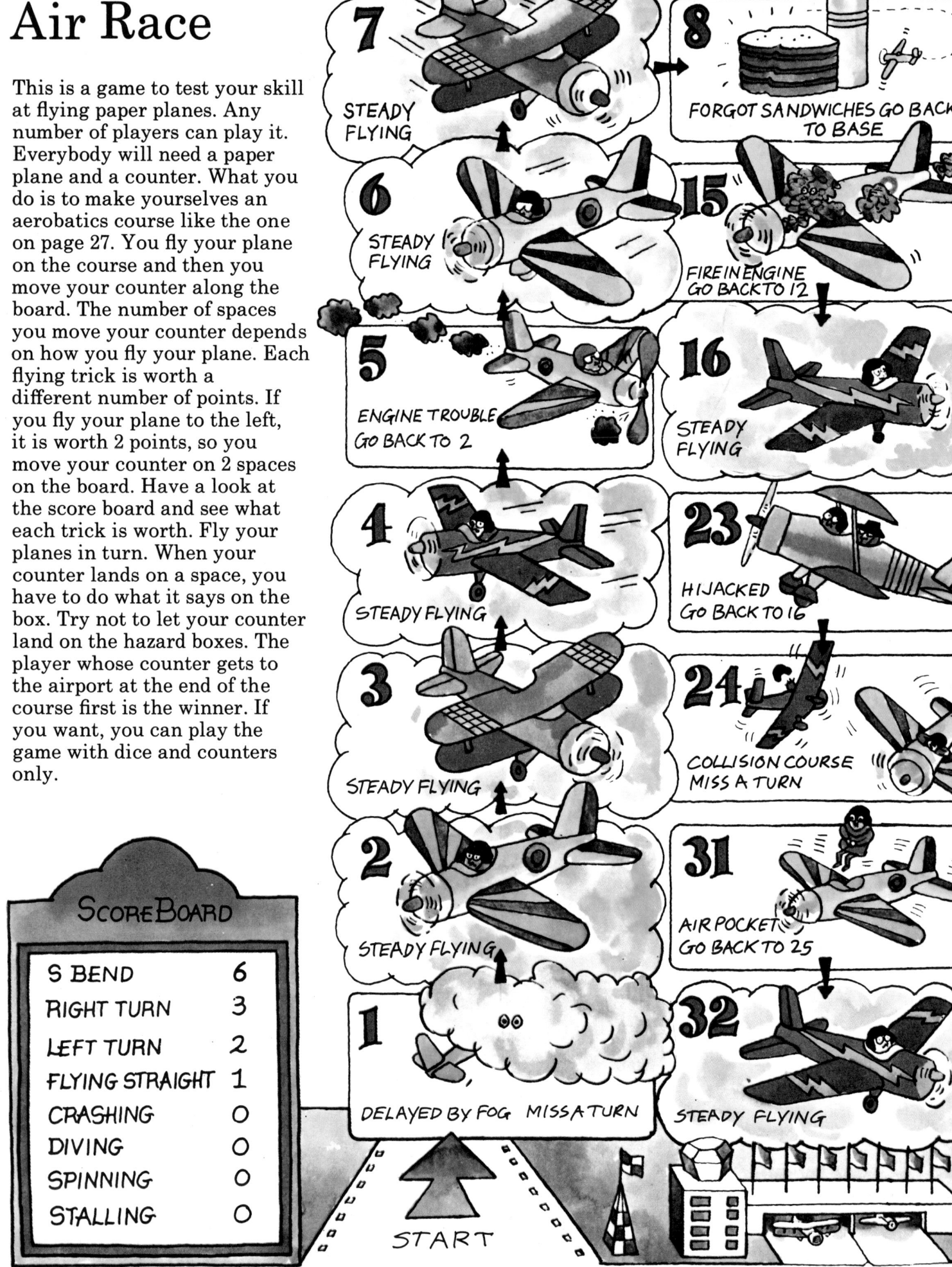

SCOREBOARD

S BEND	6
RIGHT TURN	3
LEFT TURN	2
FLYING STRAIGHT	1
CRASHING	0
DIVING	0
SPINNING	0
STALLING	0

7 STEADY FLYING

8 FORGOT SANDWICHES GO BACK TO BASE

6 STEADY FLYING

15 FIRE IN ENGINE GO BACK TO 12

5 ENGINE TROUBLE GO BACK TO 2

16 STEADY FLYING

4 STEADY FLYING

23 HIJACKED GO BACK TO 16

3 STEADY FLYING

24 COLLISION COURSE MISS A TURN

2 STEADY FLYING

31 AIR POCKET GO BACK TO 25

1 DELAYED BY FOG MISS A TURN

32 STEADY FLYING

START

Hang Gliders

One of the first aeroplanes was a Hang Glider. It was invented by a German called Otto Lilienthal in 1891. He was a very successful pioneer of flying. He had no controls on his glider. He hung by his arms under it and changed its direction by swinging his body.

You will need

a polythene bag at least
  20 × 20cm
4 drinking straws
a small, light, plastic figure
  or plasticine and a paper clip
scissors, thread and sticky tape

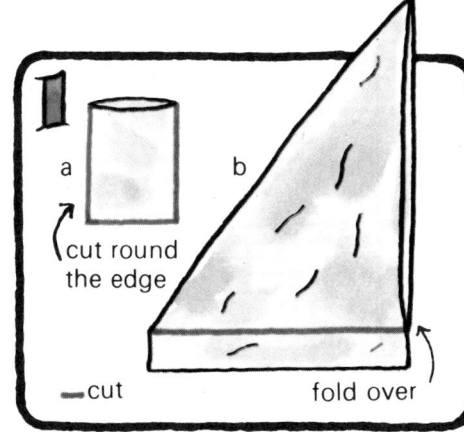

Cut round the edges of a polythene bag (a). Fold one piece as shown to make a square (b).

Tape two straws along the edge of the polythene as shown. Turn it over and tape the straws on from the other side too.

The Hang Glider

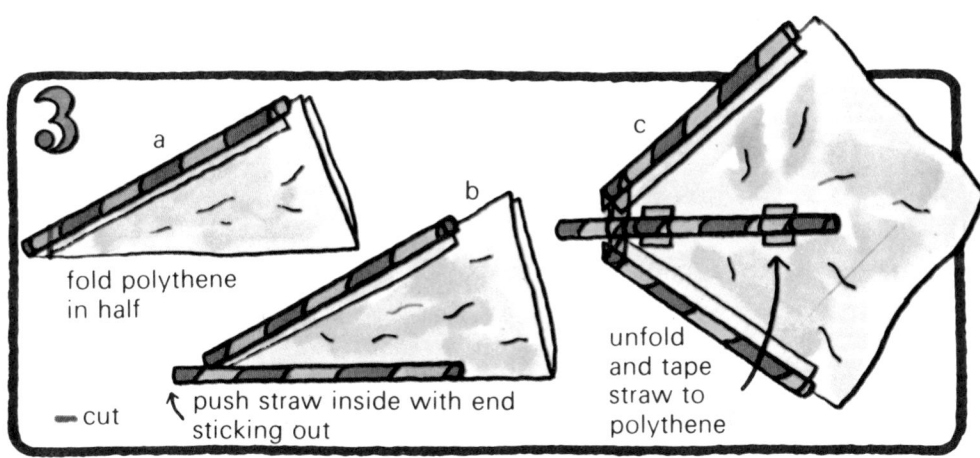
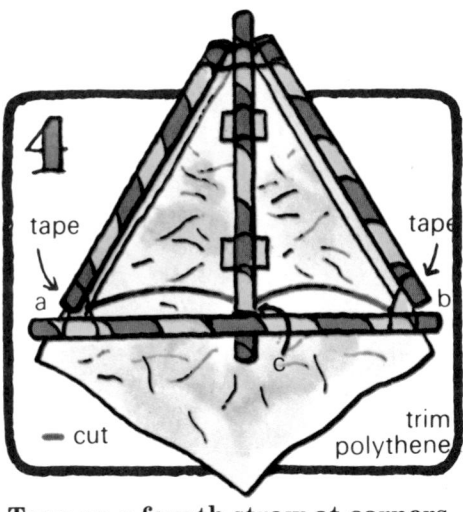

3 fold polythene in half — cut — push straw inside with end sticking out

c unfold and tape straw to polythene

4 tape / tape a / b — cut / c / trim polythene

Fold in half and snip 1 cm off its front (a). Push another straw inside the polythene with its end sticking out at the front (b).

Unfold very gently. Try to keep the third straw exactly in the middle. Then tape it on to the polythene as shown (c).

Tape on a fourth straw at corners (a) and (b) only. Trim off middle straw (c). Trim the polythene as shown.

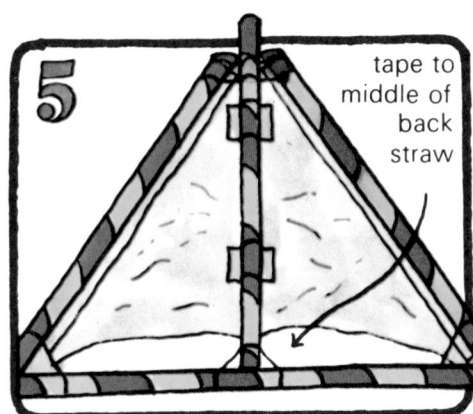

5 tape to middle of back straw

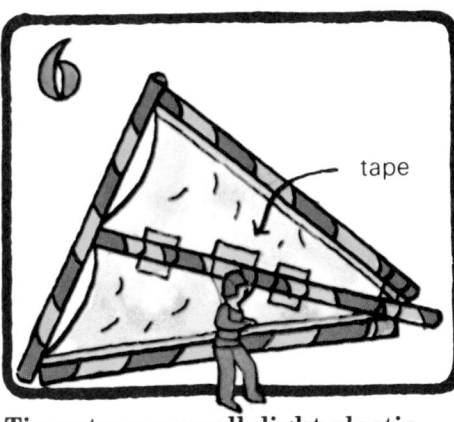

6 tape

Tape the middle straw to the fourth straw as shown. Your polythene should be a little baggy, and not taped at the back.

Tie or tape a small, light plastic figure to the centre straw as shown to balance the plane. A plasticine weighted paper clip will balance the plane if you have no toy.

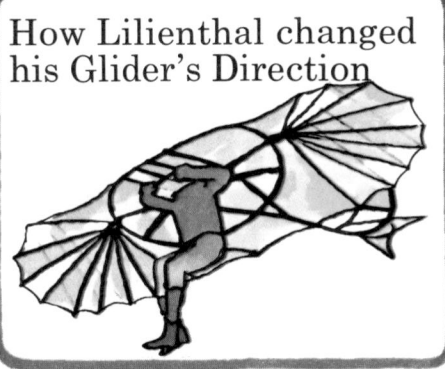

How Lilienthal changed his Glider's Direction

Lilienthal swung his body in different directions to make his glider fly differently. To raise the nose, he made the glider tail heavy by swinging his legs back.

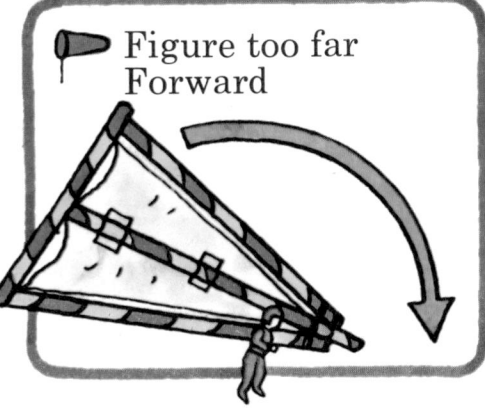

Figure too far Forward

Your glider's nose will be too heavy and the glider will dive. Move the figure back until your Hang Glider flies smoothly.

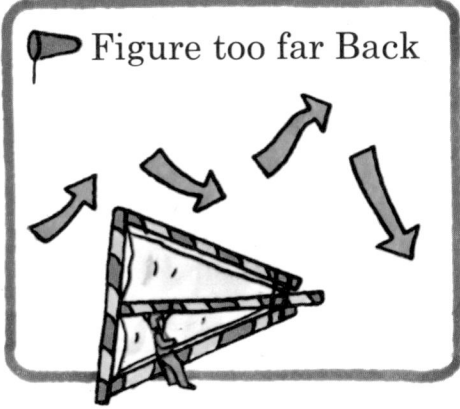

Figure too far Back

Your glider's tail will be too heavy and the glider will stall. Move the figure forward bit by bit until the plane glides smoothly.

Kites

Flying a kite can be great fun, but you may find it a bit tricky at first to keep it up in the air. Try changing the length of the tail, or tying the string on to the bridle in a different place, until your kite stays up easily. It is a good idea to wear gloves.

You will need

4 polystyrene tiles 30cm square × 7·5mm
1·30m of 7·5 × 7·5mm hardwood
8 paper fasteners size S6
a ball of thin string or nylon thread
cloth 15cm × 52cm
a paper clip and sticky tape

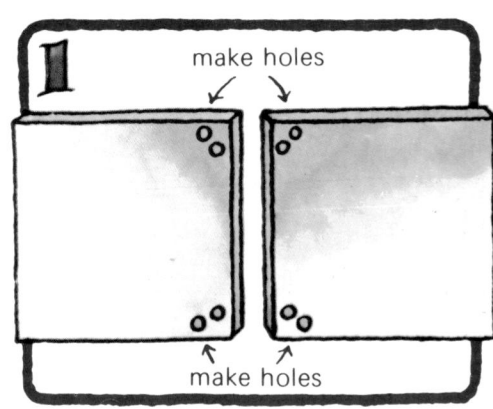

Make holes through two of the tiles with a knitting needle.

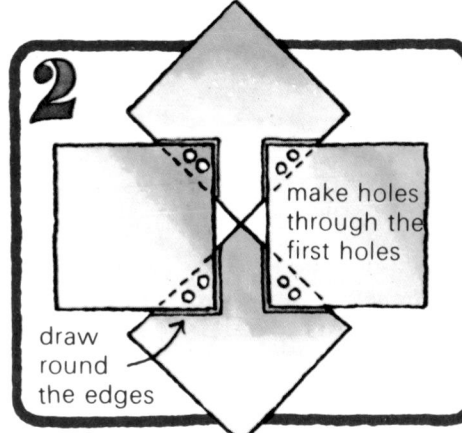

Lay the tiles out. You have to make knitting needle holes in the bottom tiles under the holes in the top tiles. Draw round the top tiles to help keep the tiles in line.

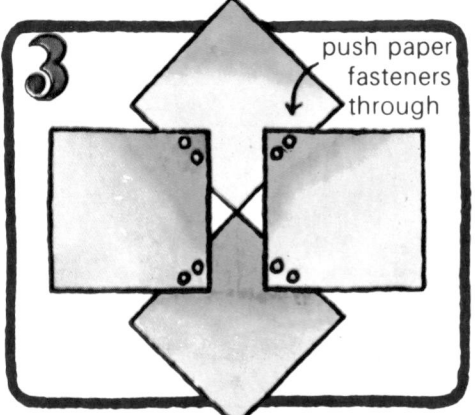

Fasten the tiles together with paper fasteners by pushing the fasteners through the holes and opening their ends out on the underside of the tiles.

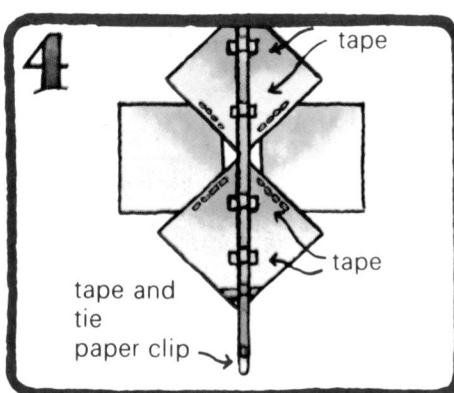

Turn the tiles over. Tape the stick right down the middle as shown. Tie and then tape a paper clip firmly to the bottom of the stick.

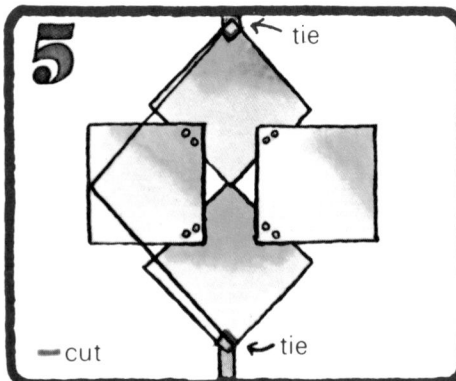

Cut two little notches in the top and bottom of the tiles as shown. Measure some string from the top notches to the side of the kite and down to the bottom notches. Tie.

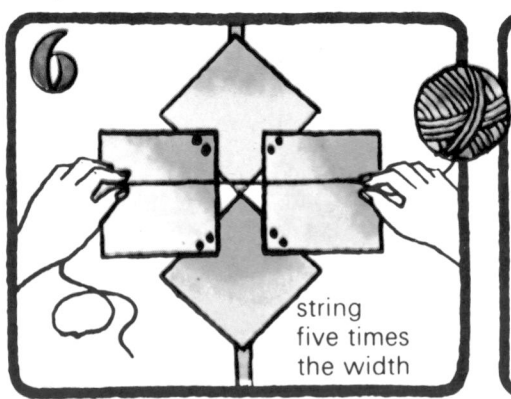

Measure a length of string five times the width of the kite and cut it. This is for the tail.

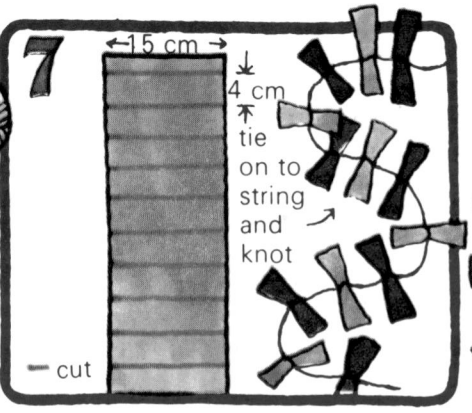

Cut the strip of cloth into about 13 strips 4 cm wide. Tie the cloth strips to the tail string as shown.

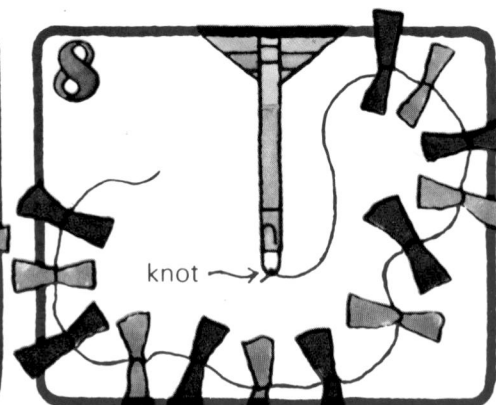

Tie the tail to the paper clip at the bottom of the stick as shown.

Flying a Kite

Stand with your back to the wind. Hold the kite so that the wind blows into it, catches it and takes it up into the air. Pay out the string bit by bit.

jerk

If there is not much wind, you may be able to get your kite into the air if you run along with it against the wind, jerking the string into the air.

If the Tail is too short

You can tell if the kite's tail is too short because the kite will rise a little and then spin round and round. You will have to make the tail longer.

Looking after the Tail

Sometimes the tail may get very tangled when you are not using the kite. Wrap the tail around a cardboard tube when you put the kite away.

9 tie to bridle $\frac{1}{3}$ of way down

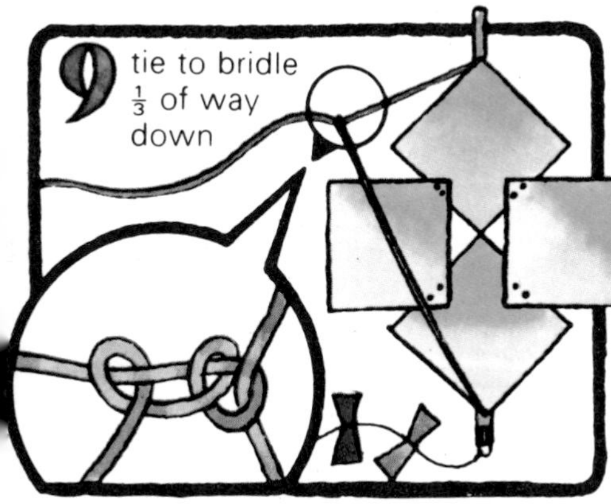

The string tied to the kite is called the bridle. Tie the end of your ball of string about $\frac{1}{3}$ of the way from the top of the bridle. Tie it with a knot like this.

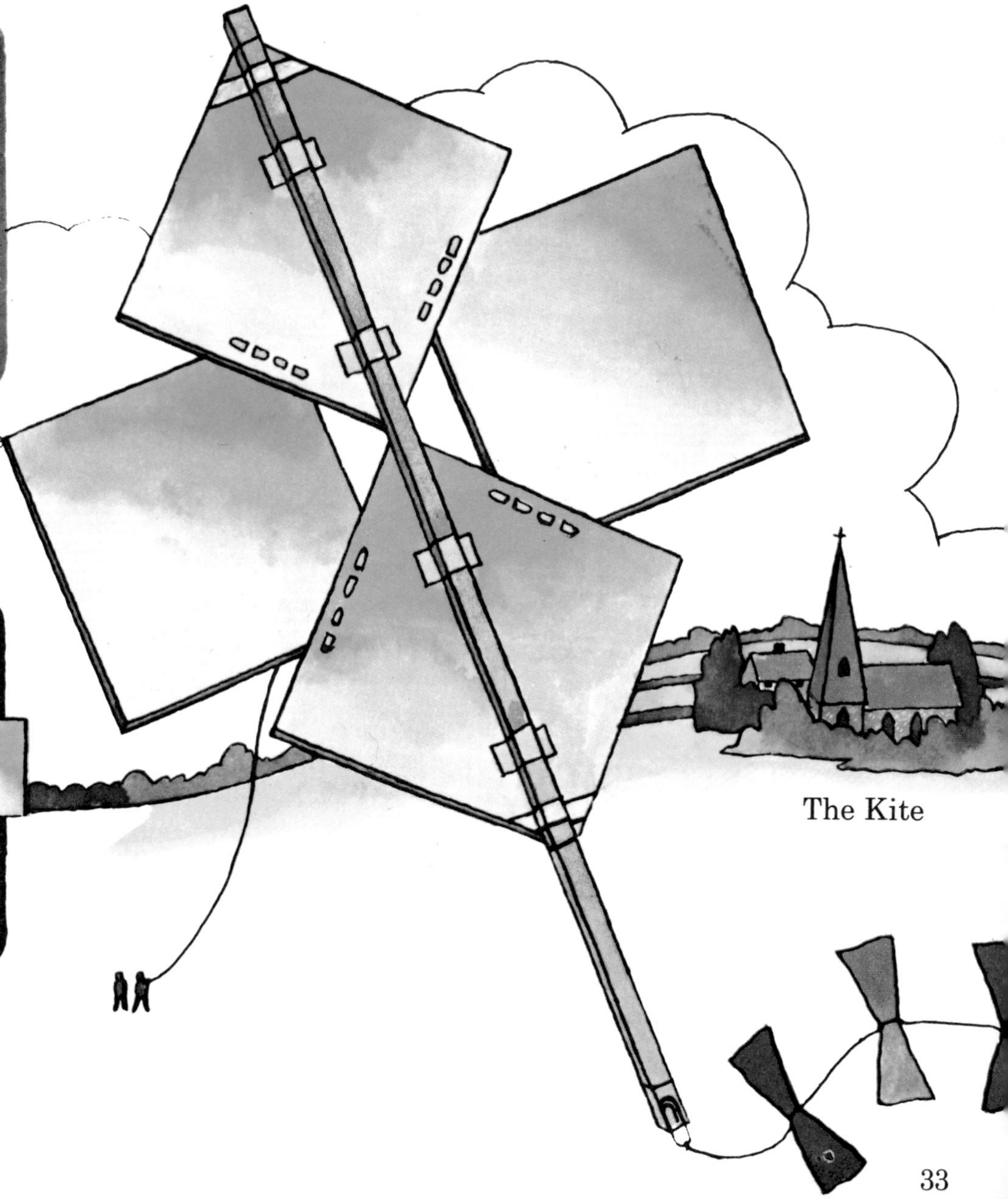

The Kite

The KnowHow Anemometer

Anemometers tell you how hard the wind is blowing. The work comes from the Greek word Anemos, which means wind.

You will need
thick card 20cm × 7cm
card from a document folder
a sheet of paper 21cm × 29cm
2 drinking straws
a round ball point pen top
a knitting needle
a darning needle
an empty cream or yoghurt carton
30cm thread
sticky tape and strong glue
magic marker

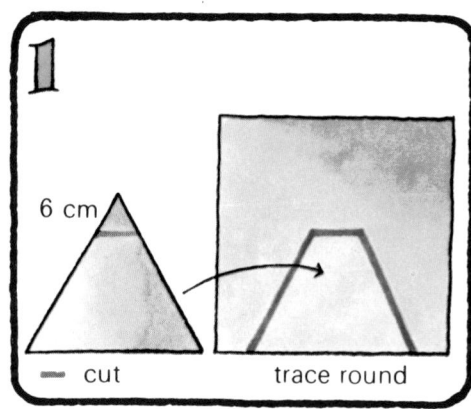

Cut out a triangle of thick card about 6 cm high. Cut 1 cm off the top. Put this shape on top of some more card, trace round it and cut the traced outline out.

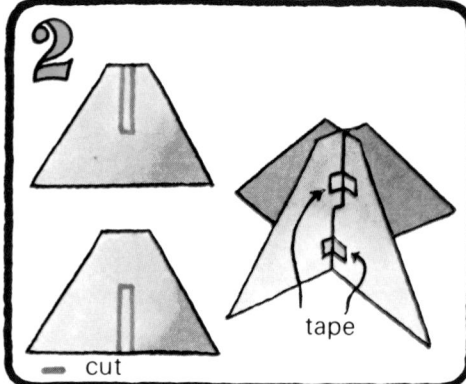

Cut a 3 cm slit in the top of the first bit of card. Cut a 3 cm slit in the bottom of the other. Slip the second shape over the first shape and tape it as shown.

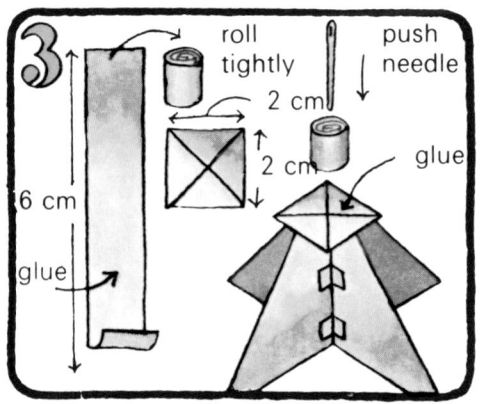

Cut some thin card into a strip. Put glue on it, roll it up tightly. Cut out a square of thin card. Glue them on to the card base as shown. Push the needle in on top.

To make four circles, fold the paper in four and draw round something the same size and shape as a cream carton. Cut the circles out, paint one of them any colour.

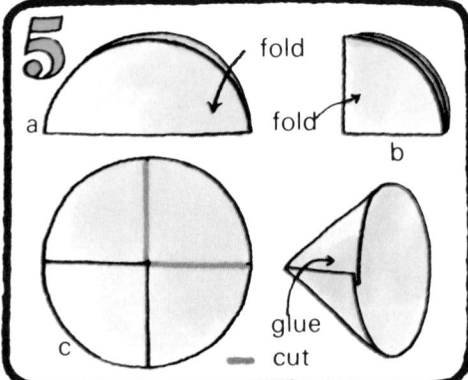

Fold each circle in half (a) and in half again (b). Open them out. Cut out a quarter as shown (c). Glue the straight edges together to make a cone.

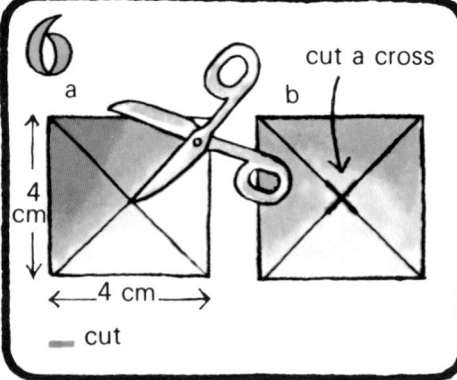

Cut out another square of strong card. Join the corners to make a cross and make a hole in the middle with your scissors (a). Cut a small cross as shown (b).

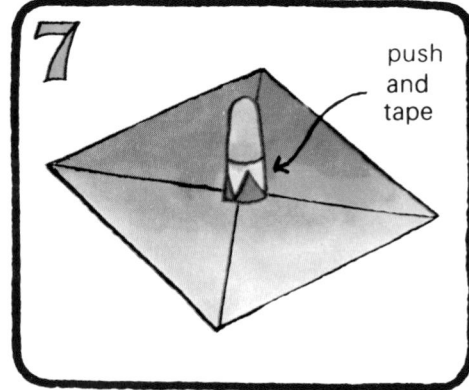

Push the pen top through the card square and tape it firmly on to the bits of card sticking up as shown.

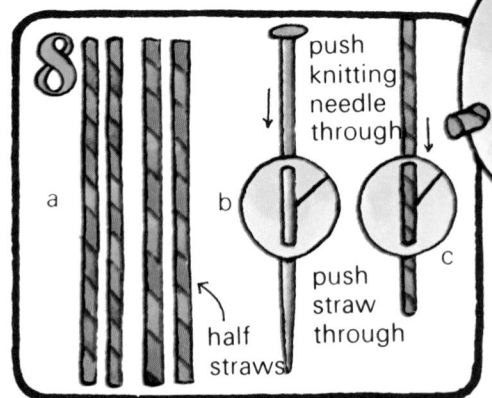

Cut two straws in half to make four half straws (a). Make holes in your four cones with a knitting needle (b). Push your half straws through the holes as shown (c).

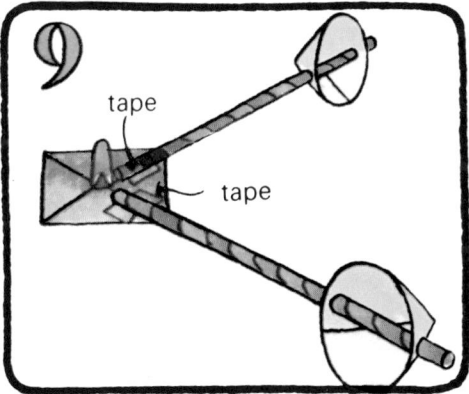

Tape each half straw with its cone on to the card square as shown. Make sure that the pointed end of each cone points towards the open end of the one before.

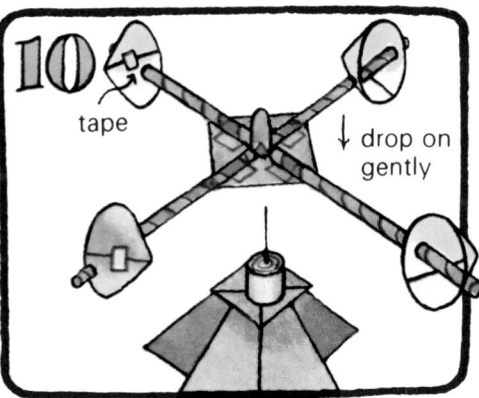

Hold the top of the ball point pen top and drop the whole thing on to the darning needle on the card base as shown.

Working an Anemometer

Put your anemometer on the ground outside. The wind will blow into the open end of the cones and push them round. See how many times the coloured cone passes you while you slowly count one Know-How, two KnowHow, three, up to five. The number of times this cone passes you will give you a wind count. The higher the wind count, the harder the wind is blowing. If you try this on different days, you can find out what wind count is good for flying planes out of doors and what wind count is too high for them.

If you want to, you can do it another way. Cut 30 cm of thread. Knot the ends. Cut two slits as shown. Slip a knot under each slit. Put the anemometer outside, hold the thread up and count. The thread will wind up as the cones go round. When you have counted up to five, wind the cones round the opposite way to the way the wind blew them until the thread is completely unwound. The number of times the coloured cone passes you will be the wind count. Try doing it this way if the wind is blowing very hard.

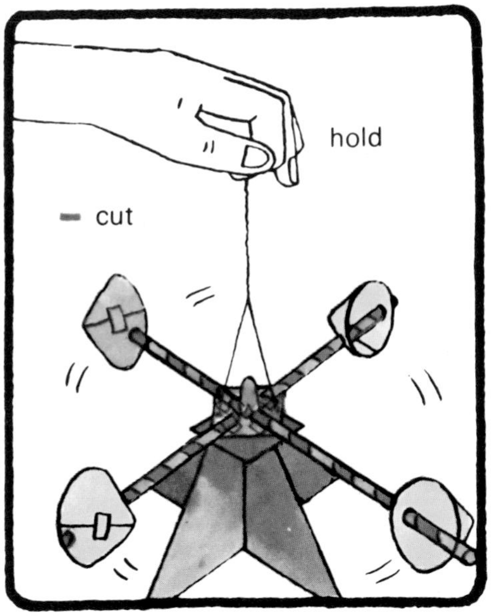

The Anemometer going round in a wind

35

The KnowHow Balance

The KnowHow Balance is a Plane Tester. You use it to find out if your plane is going to fly properly. If you cannot get your plane to balance, you will have to alter the tail or nose to make the plane less tail or nose heavy. If your plane balances properly, it should fly well. Use it to weigh paper planes too.

You will need

a cardboard box about
   12×9cm
a darning needle and paper clip
card from the back of a note pad
a straw, a pencil and ruler
  scissors and thread

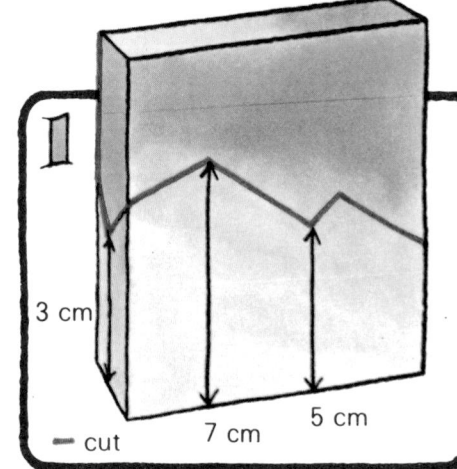

Cut two sides of the cardboard box into a shape like this.

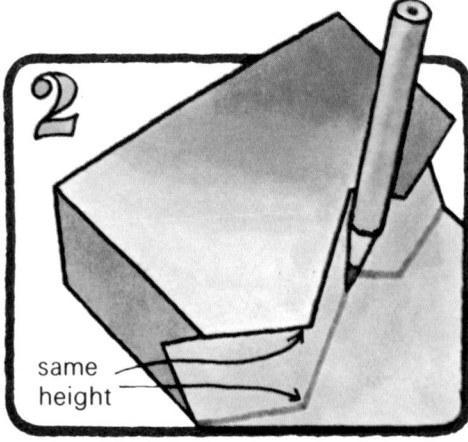

Put the box down on its side. Lean a pencil against the shape you have cut and draw the shape on the other side of the box. Cut these sides out.

The KnowHow Balance

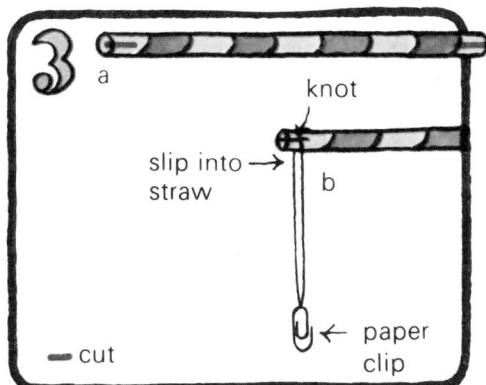

Cut slits into both ends of a straw (a). Hang a paper clip from about 24 cm of thread, knot the thread and slip it into one of the straw slits like this (b).

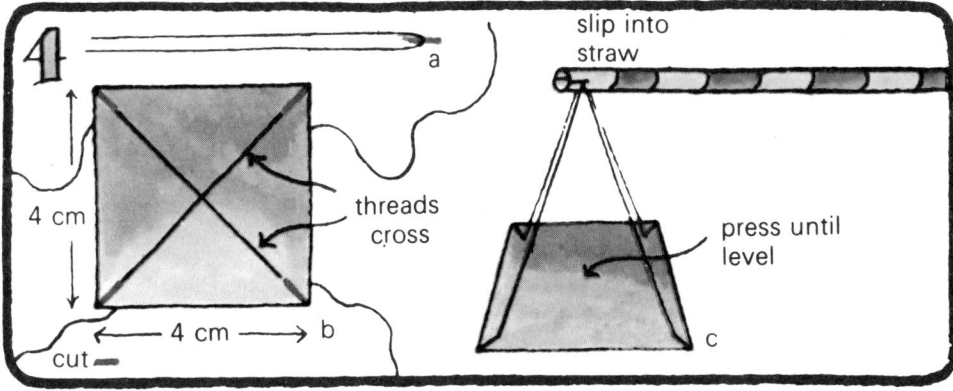

Cut about 30 cm of thread in half (a). Cut out a card square 4 cm × 4 cm and cut a slit into each corner as shown. Slip the threads into the slits so that they cross (b).

Turn the card over, knot the threads together and slip them into the other straw slit. Press the card until it is level (c).

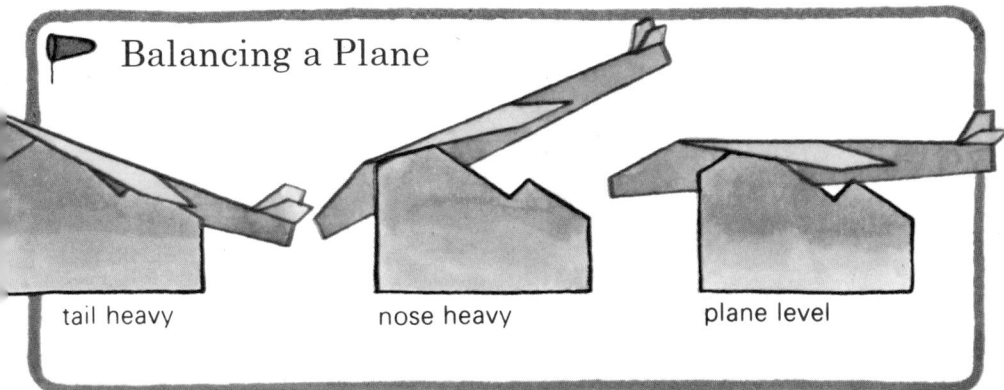

Balancing a Plane

Put your plane into the box and try to get it to balance on its wings so that it is level. If it will not balance, it is either tail heavy or nose heavy.

Put paper clips, plasticine or other weights on to the tail or nose until the plane balances well.

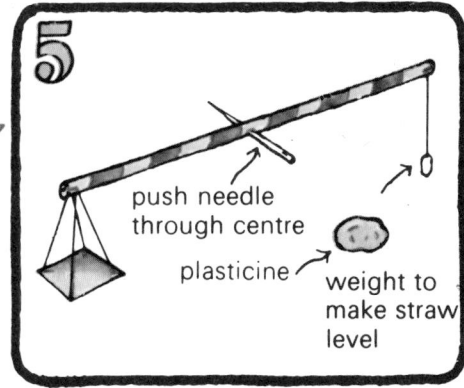

Push a darning needle through the centre of the straw. Hold the needle and see if the straw is level. Weight either the paper clip or card until both sides balance.

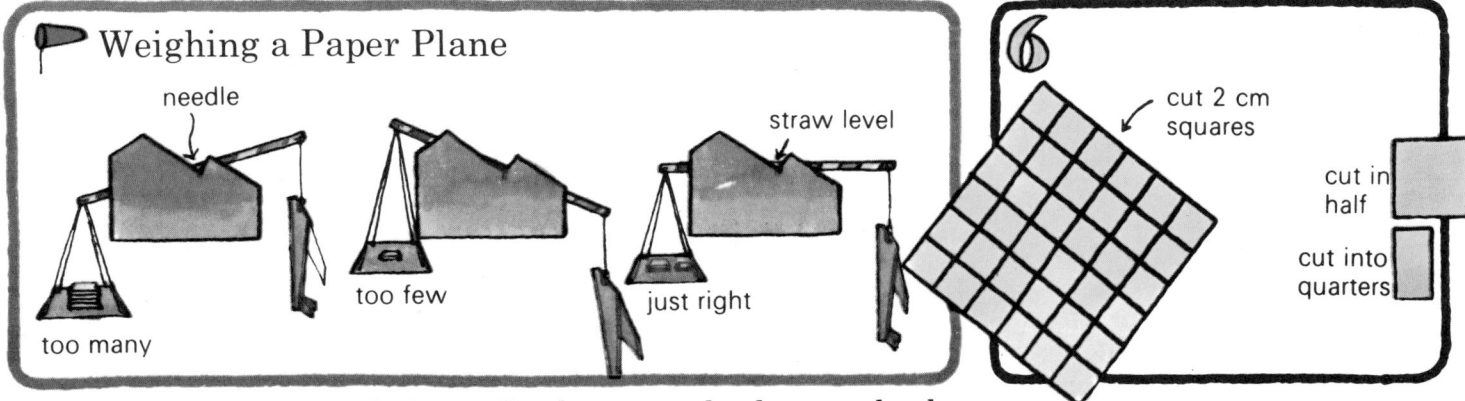

Weighing a Paper Plane

Put the straw balance into the box like this. Hang a paper plane from the paper clip. Put the card squares on to the card one by one.

You have to make the straw level by putting the right number of squares on to the card. Then count the squares and mark the number on the plane.

Cut the card from the back of a note pad into lots of squares 2 cm × 2 cm. Cut eight of these in half. Cut some of these into quarters as shown.

The KnowHow Launcher

Aeroplanes launched from the KnowHow Launcher will fly in a very smooth, straight glide. Your aeroplanes will fly very well if you hold the launcher level when you are launching them.

For the Launcher you will need

a cardboard tube 30cm × 3·5cm
2 knitting needles size 8, 35cm long
2, 13cm rubber bands 1·5mm thick or a piece of elastic
a piece of strong card (the back of a writing pad)
30cm of string
2 paper clips
a small wheel without a tyre from an old toy car
scissors and a ruler
sticky tape and strong glue

If you want, you can put it on to a launching pad and turn it into a Missile Launcher.

You will need

a shoe box (about 30cm × 9cm)
a smaller box (about 15cm × 12cm)
a ball point pen top
2 paper fasteners

Put the Launcher on a flat surface to launch planes.

1 Making the Launcher

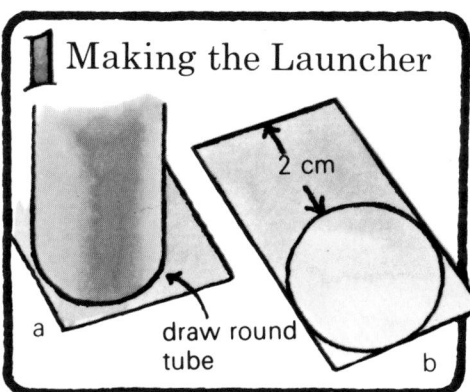

2 cm

a — draw round tube — b

Put the tube in the corner of the strong card. Draw round it (a). Take the tube away and cut out a shape like this (b) with the circle on it. Do the same again.

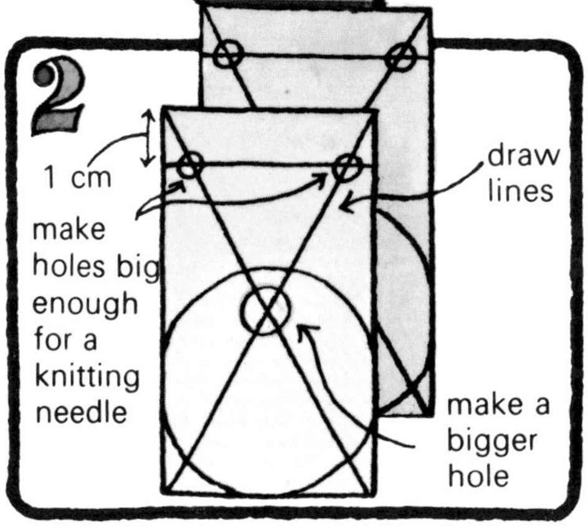

2

1 cm

make holes big enough for a knitting needle

draw lines

make a bigger hole

Draw lines on both the shapes to join the corners up. Draw another line about 1 cm from the top of both. Make holes as shown.

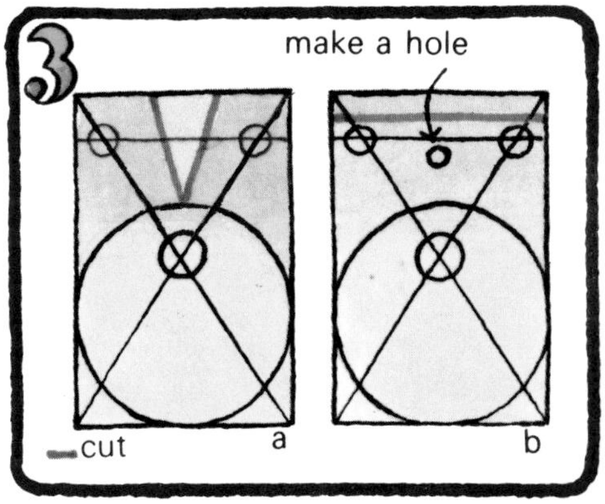

3

make a hole

cut — a   b

Cut a notch in the top of one of the shapes (a). Cut straight across the other just above the holes. Make a fourth hole in this piece only as shown (b).

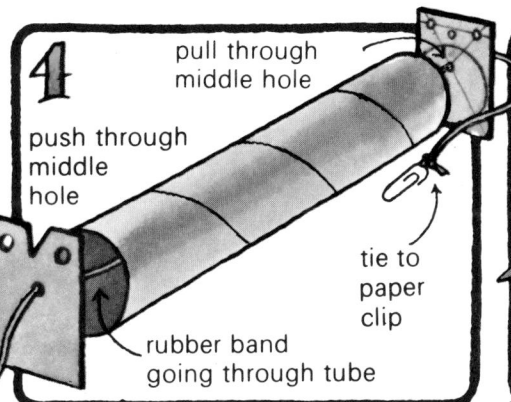

4 pull through middle hole / push through middle hole / tie to paper clip / rubber band going through tube

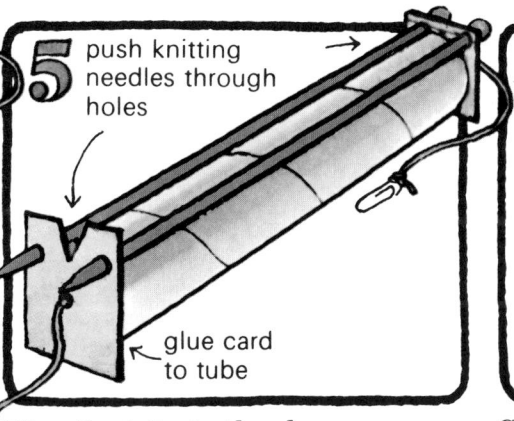

5 push knitting needles through holes / glue card to tube

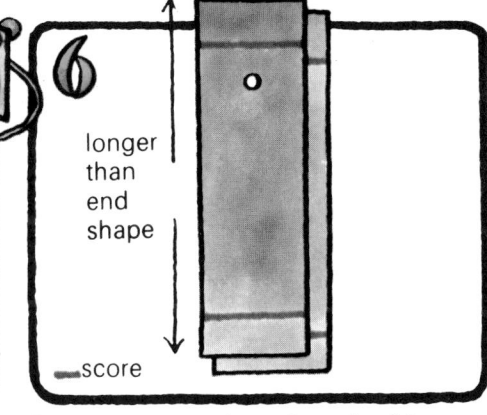

6 longer than end shape / score

Snip open two rubber bands and tie them together to make one long piece. Tie a paper clip to one end. Push the other end through the shapes and tube as shown.

Glue the tube to the shapes over the circles you have drawn on them. Push two knitting needles through the top holes as shown.

Cut out two strips of card a bit longer than the end shapes. Score them as shown. Make a hole in them both in the same place as shown.

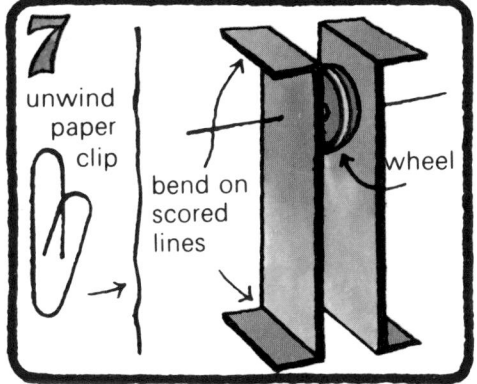

7 unwind paper clip / bend on scored lines / wheel

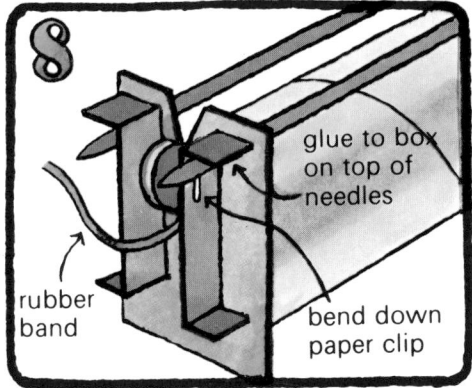

8 glue to box on top of needles / rubber band / bend down paper clip

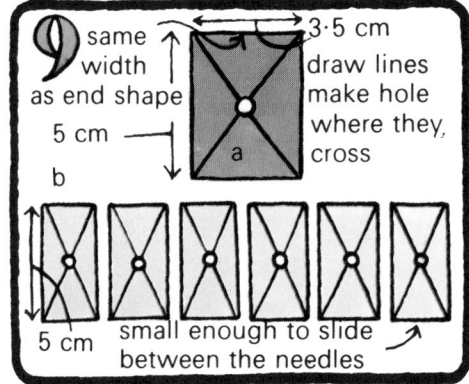

9 same width as end shape / 3·5 cm / draw lines make hole where they cross / 5 cm / b / a / 5 cm / small enough to slide between the needles

Unwind the paper clip. Bend the card strips like this. Push the paper clip through the strips and the wheel as shown.

Glue the strips on to the end shape with the free end of the rubber band as shown. Bend both ends of the paper clip down.

Cut out one bit of card 3·5 × 5 cm (a). Cut out six bits of card 1·5 × 5 cm (b). Draw lines as shown to make a cross. Make a hole in each bit of card where shown.

10 glue them on top of each other / bigger card first

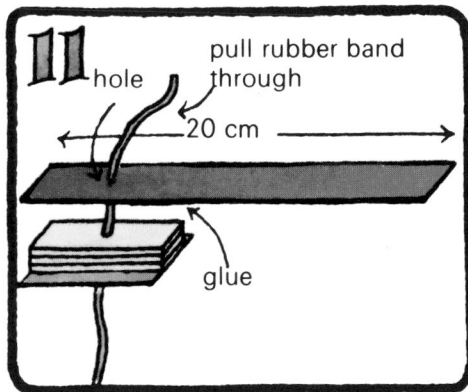

11 hole / pull rubber band through / 20 cm / glue

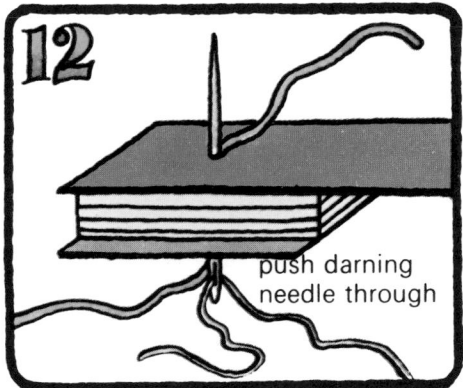

12 push darning needle through

Push the free end of the rubber band through the hole in the bigger card and then through the holes in the smaller cards. Glue them on top of each other.

Cut out a strip of card 5 cm × 20 cm. Make a hole in this strip where shown. Pull the rubber band through and glue this strip on to the other bits of card as shown.

Cut a length of string 30 cm long. Thread it through a darning needle and push the needle through the hole in the card block as shown.

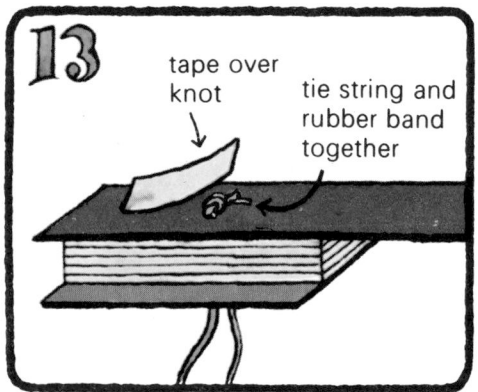

13 tape over knot · tie string and rubber band together

Unthread the needle and string and tie the string and rubber band together as shown. Put some tape over the knot.

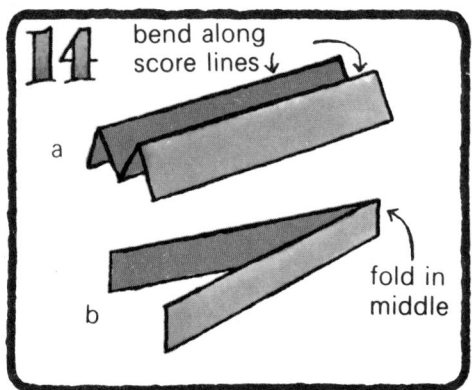

14 bend along score lines ↓ · a · b · fold in middle

Cut out a piece of card 15 cm × 4 cm Score it and bend it into this shape (a). Cut out another piece of card 20 cm long and fold it in half as shown (b).

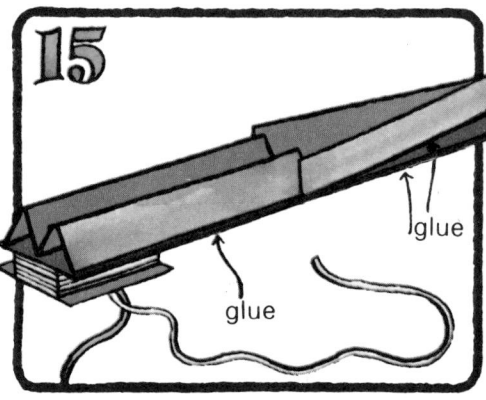

15 glue · glue

Glue both the pieces of card on to the top of the card block as shown.

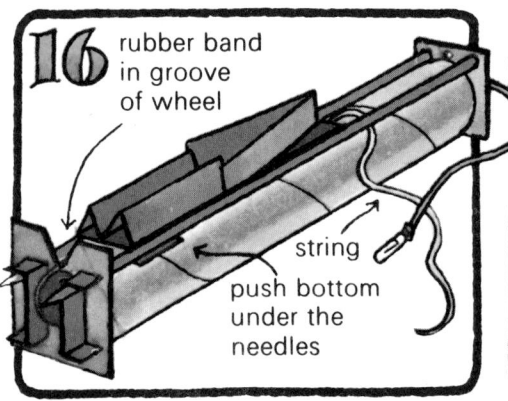

16 rubber band in groove of wheel · string · push bottom under the needles

Push the bottom card of the card block under the knitting needle rails so that the card block can slide up and down the needle rails easily.

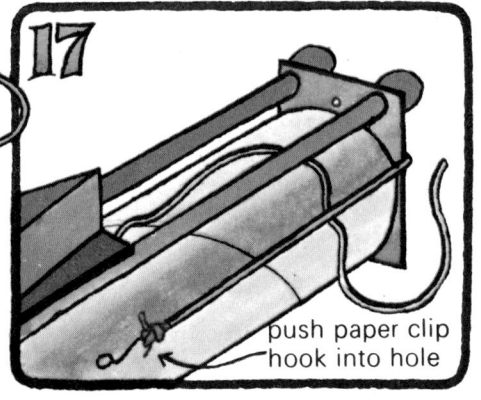

17 push paper clip hook into hole

Pull the rubber band at the other end of the launcher along the tube until it is tight. Make a hole in the tube, bend the paper clip into a hook and hook it into the hole.

18 string must not sag · push string through button · tie a knot near launcher

Thread the string through the hole at the back of the launcher and through a button. Pull it tight, but not so that the card block slides back and knot it as shown.

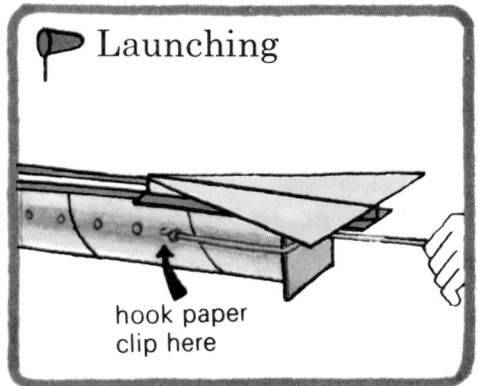

⚑ Launching

hook paper clip here

Put the plane on to the launching pad like this. Pull the string loop as far back as you can. Then, let the loop go.

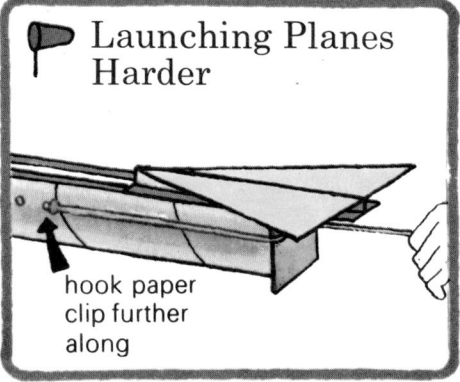

⚑ Launching Planes Harder

hook paper clip further along

If you want to launch planes harder, make more holes along the tube as shown. Hook the rubber band and paper clip into the different holes.

⚑ Do not Launch them too hard

Gliders like the Drinking Straw Glider will not fly well if you launch them too hard. Put the hook into different holes until the plane glides smoothly.

Missile Launcher

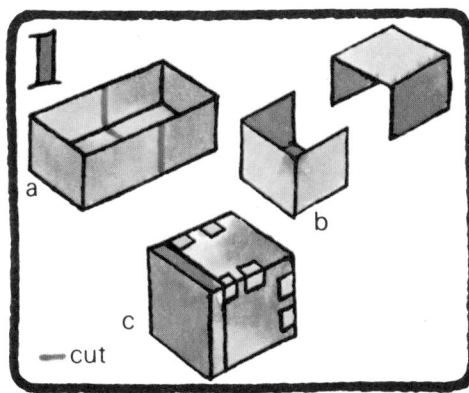

1

a

b

c

cut

Cut the bottom of a shoe box in half (a). Turn one half upside down (b) and tape it into the other half as shown (c).

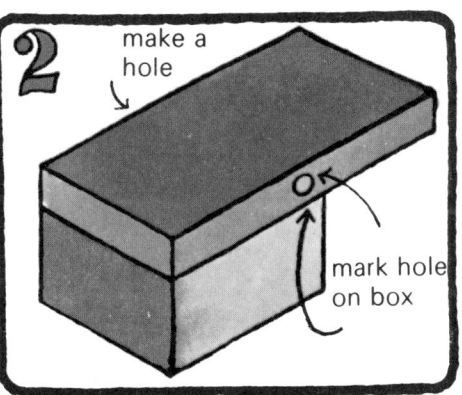

2 make a hole

mark hole on box

Put the lid on to the box and make two holes where shown. Make pencil marks through these holes on to the box.

3 paper fastener ends bent inside box

Take the lid off and make two more holes on the pencil marks. Put the lid on, push a paper fastener through both holes. Bend its ends inside the box.

If you want, you can turn the launcher into a Missile Launcher by putting it on to a missile launching pad like the one here. Look at page 38 for what you will need to make it.

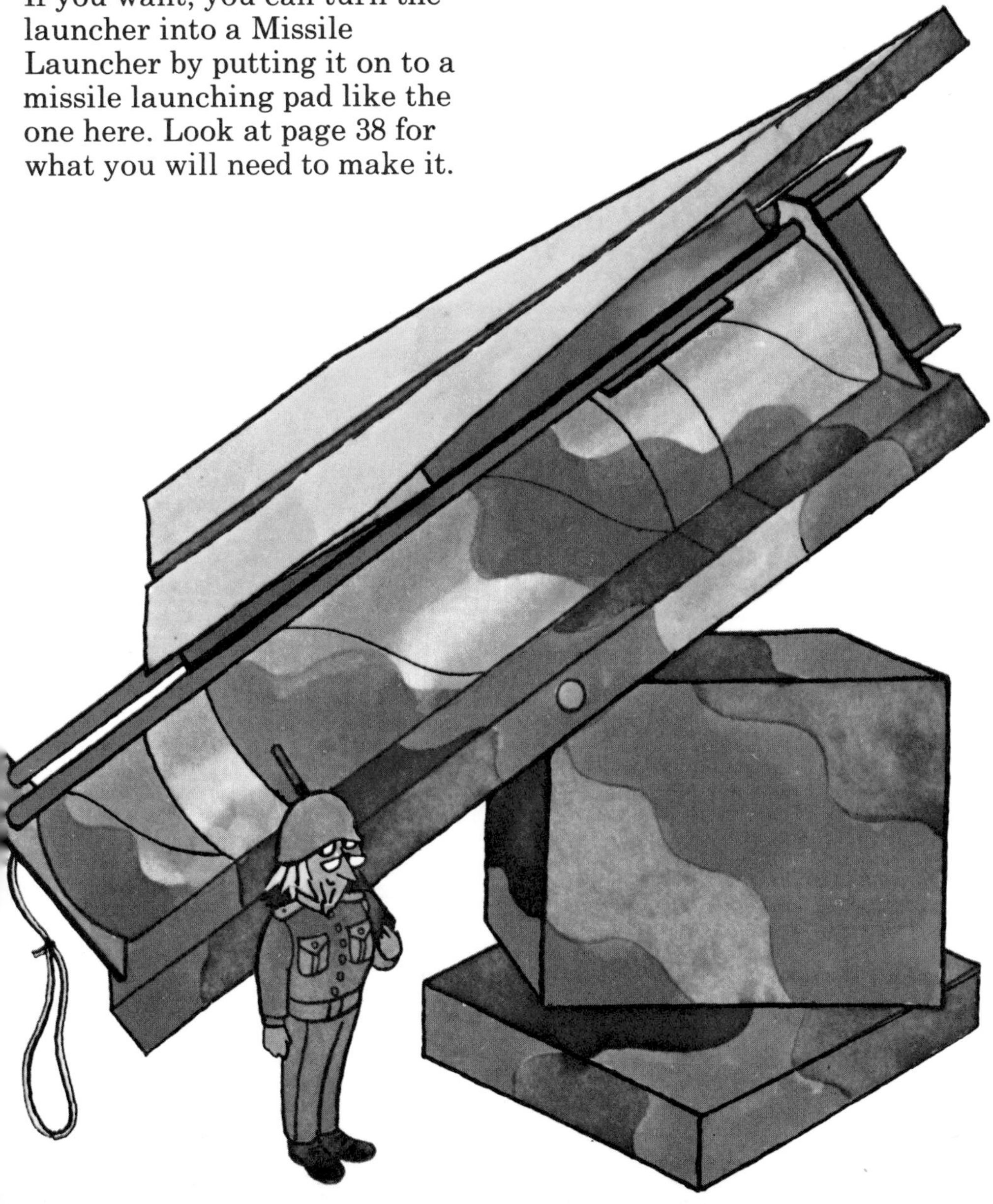

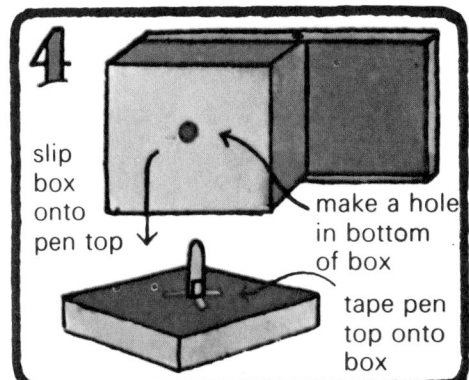

4 slip box onto pen top

make a hole in bottom of box

tape pen top onto box

Tape the ball point pen top on to the top of another box. Make a hole in the bottom of the shoe box, slip it on to the pen top.
Make the shoe box swivel round.

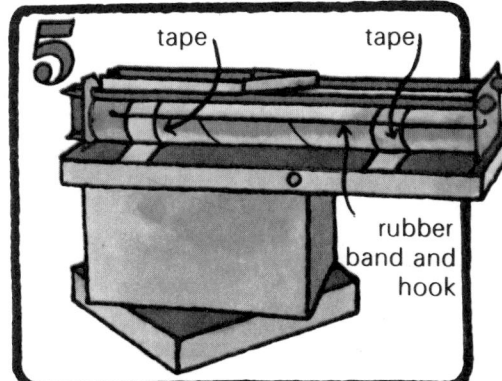

5 tape tape

rubber band and hook

Tape the launcher on to the top of the shoe box. Put the tape under both the string and rubber band. Put the hook into a hole right at the front of the launcher.

41

Patterns for Tracing

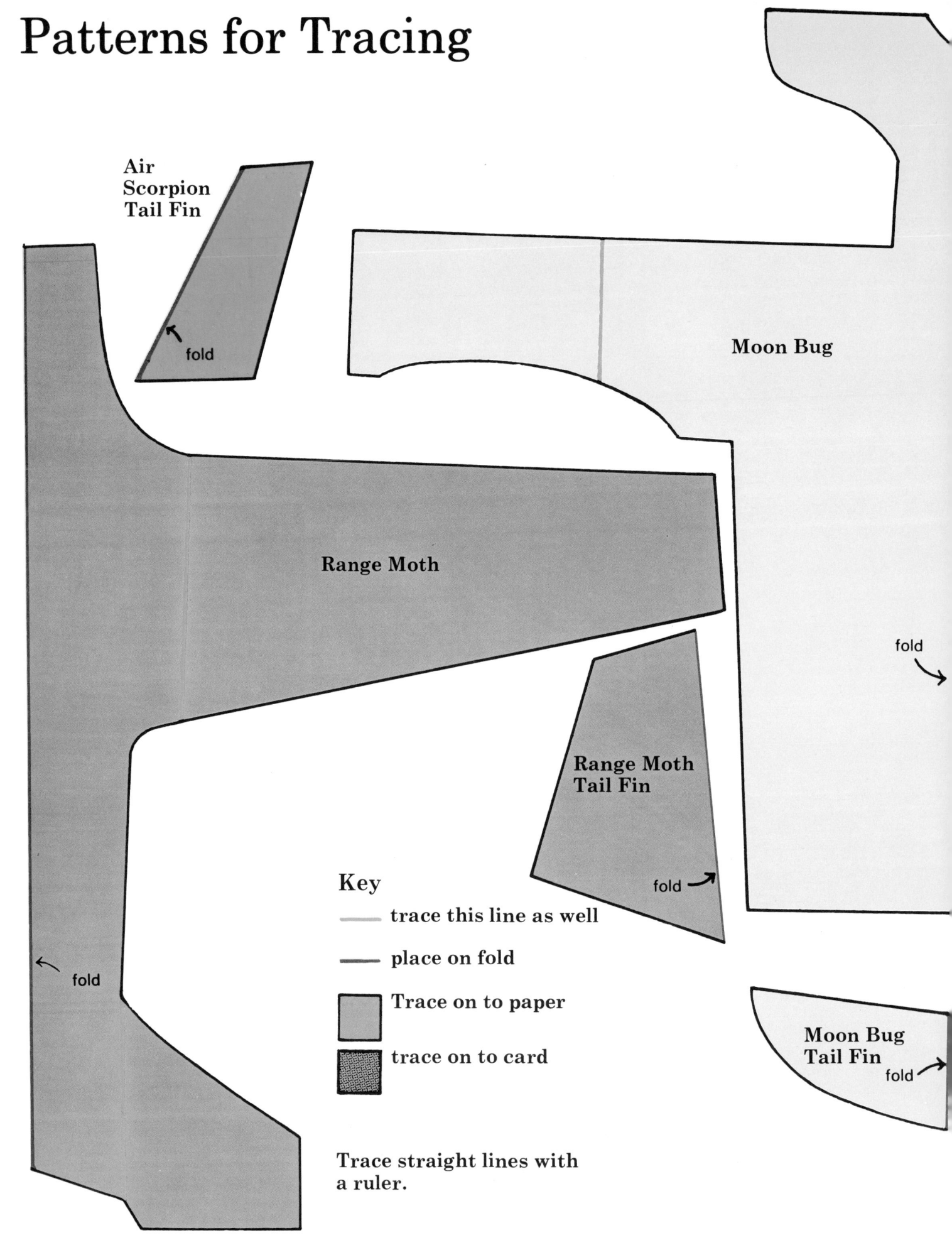

Air Scorpion Tail Fin

fold

Moon Bug

fold

Range Moth

Range Moth Tail Fin

fold

fold

Key

— trace this line as well

— place on fold

Trace on to paper

trace on to card

Moon Bug Tail Fin

fold

Trace straight lines with a ruler.

42

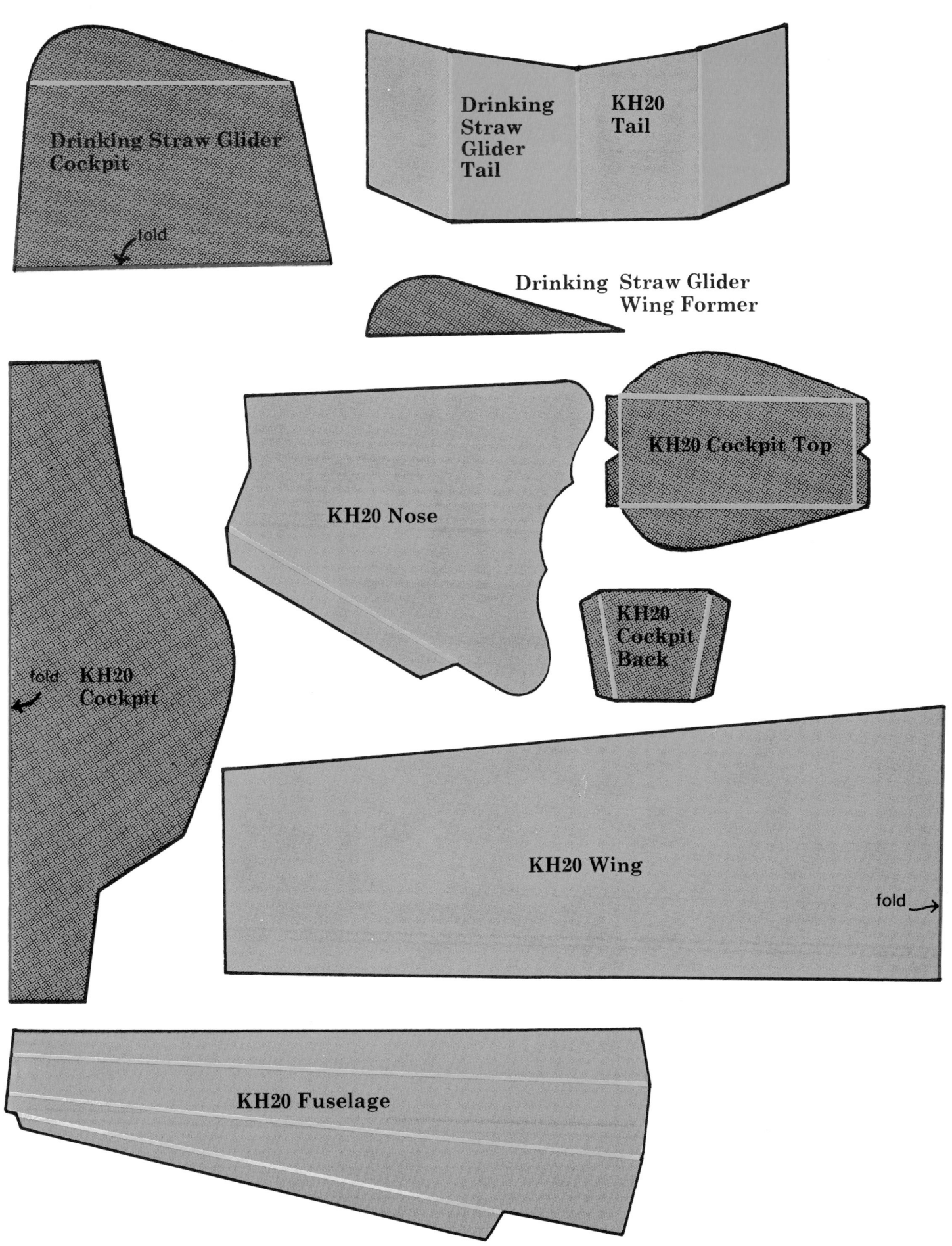

Drinking Straw Glider Cockpit

Drinking Straw Glider Tail

KH20 Tail

fold

Drinking Straw Glider Wing Former

KH20 Cockpit Top

KH20 Nose

KH20 Cockpit Back

fold KH20 Cockpit

KH20 Wing

fold

KH20 Fuselage

Patterns for Tracing
Hawkeye Devastator

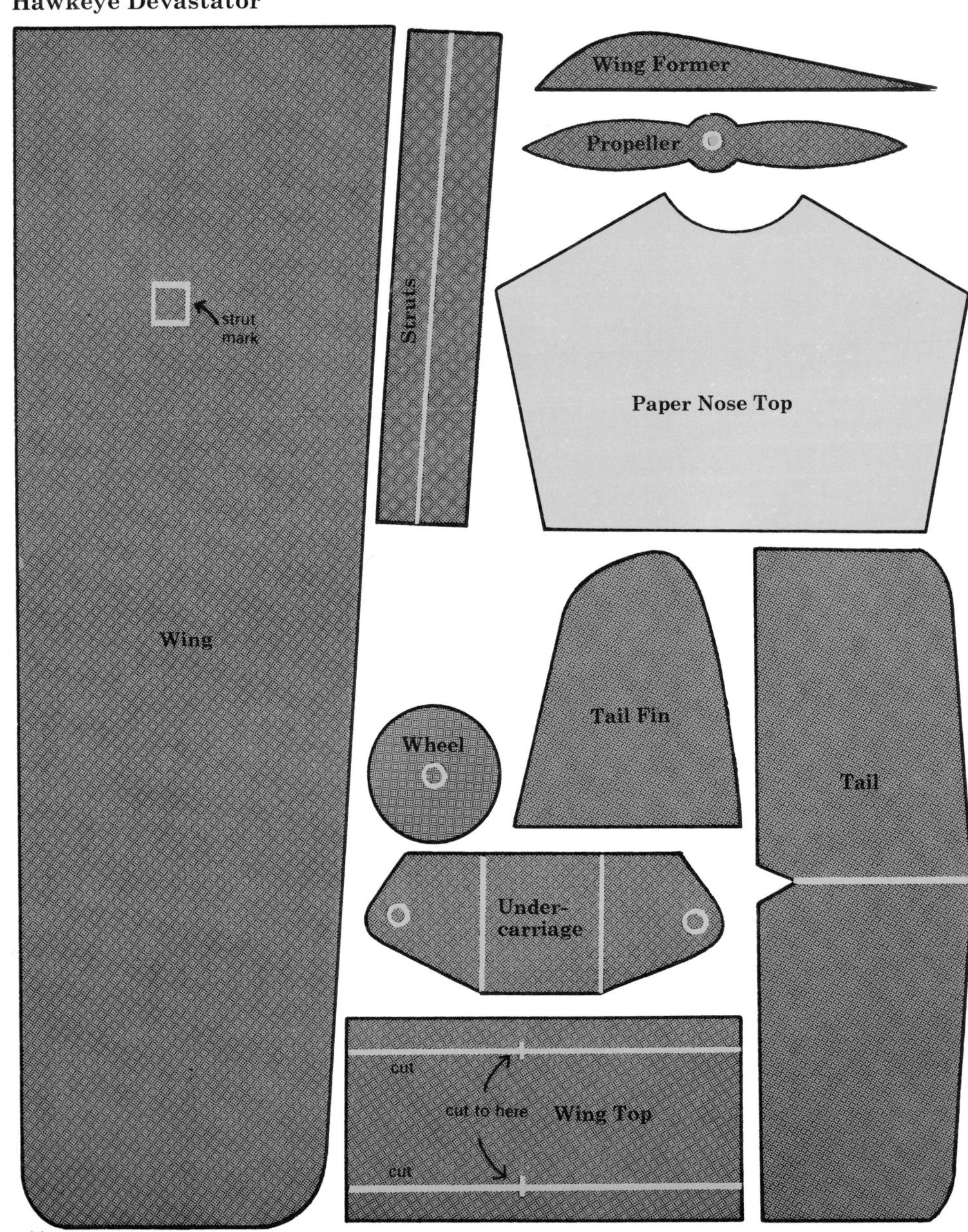

Wing

strut mark

Struts

Wing Former

Propeller

Paper Nose Top

Wheel

Tail Fin

Tail

Under-carriage

cut

cut to here

cut

Wing Top

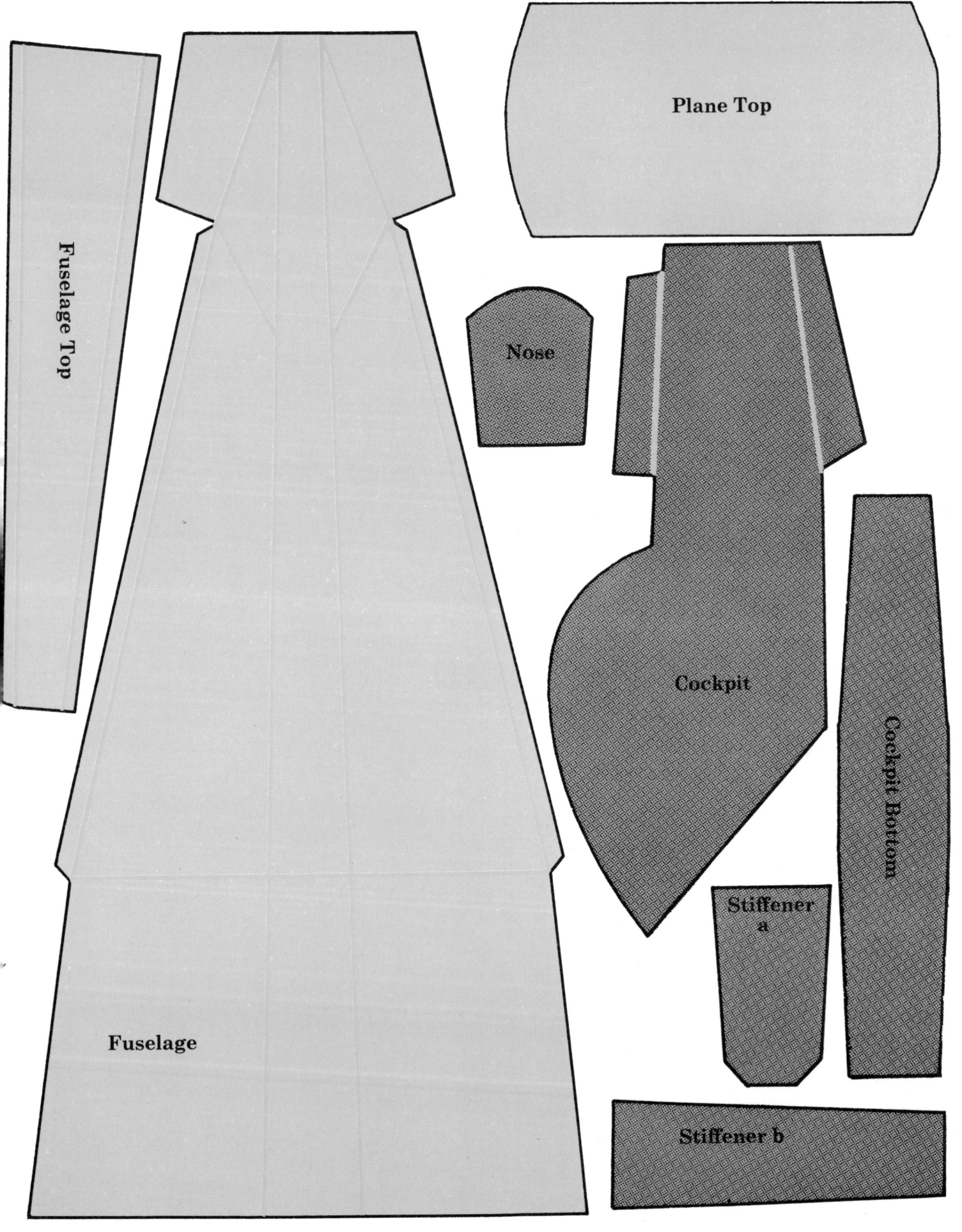

Fuselage Top

Plane Top

Nose

Cockpit

Cockpit Bottom

Stiffener a

Fuselage

Stiffener b

Going Further

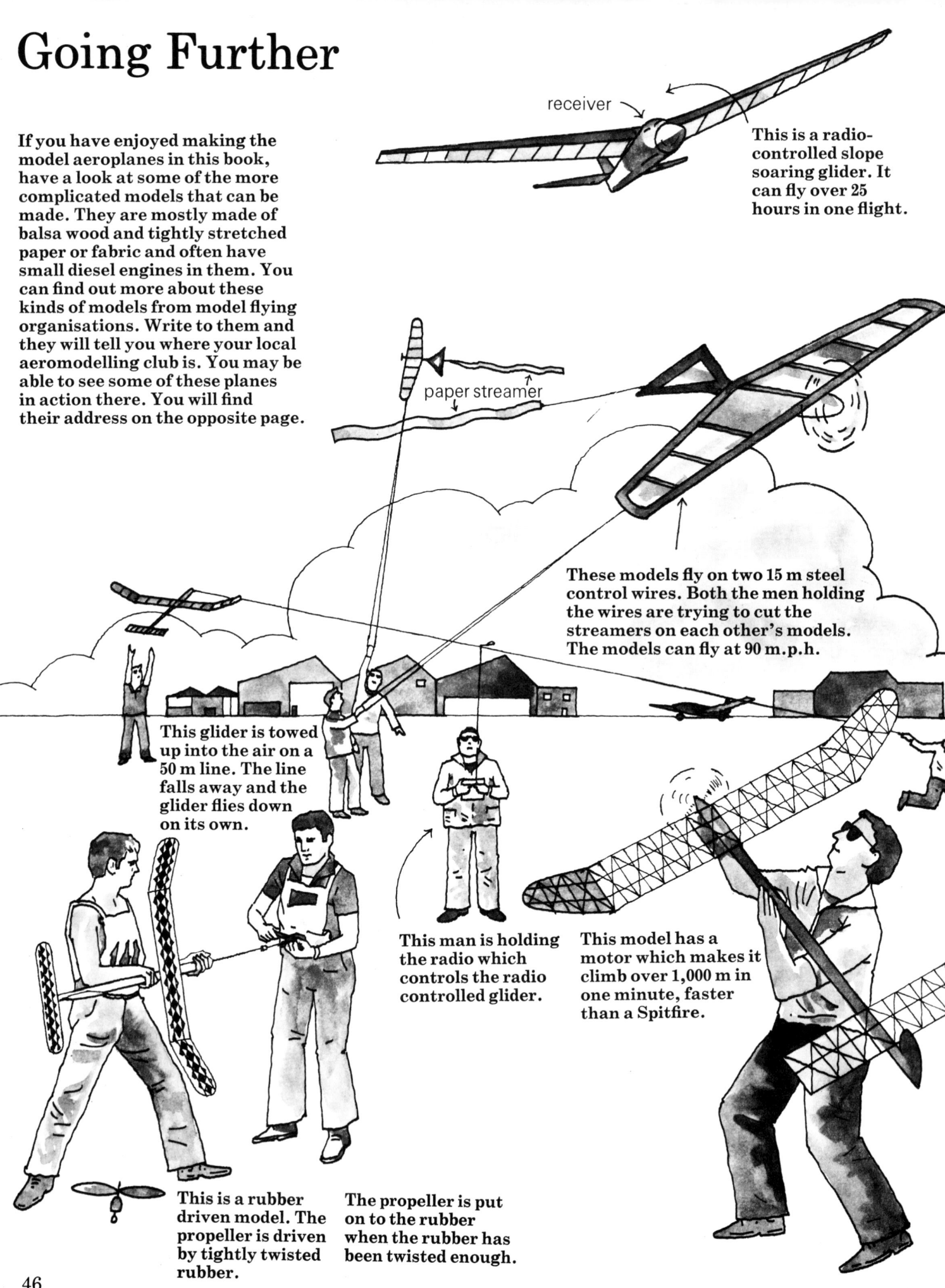

If you have enjoyed making the model aeroplanes in this book, have a look at some of the more complicated models that can be made. They are mostly made of balsa wood and tightly stretched paper or fabric and often have small diesel engines in them. You can find out more about these kinds of models from model flying organisations. Write to them and they will tell you where your local aeromodelling club is. You may be able to see some of these planes in action there. You will find their address on the opposite page.

receiver

This is a radio-controlled slope soaring glider. It can fly over 25 hours in one flight.

paper streamer

These models fly on two 15 m steel control wires. Both the men holding the wires are trying to cut the streamers on each other's models. The models can fly at 90 m.p.h.

This glider is towed up into the air on a 50 m line. The line falls away and the glider flies down on its own.

This man is holding the radio which controls the radio controlled glider.

This model has a motor which makes it climb over 1,000 m in one minute, faster than a Spitfire.

This is a rubber driven model. The propeller is driven by tightly twisted rubber.

The propeller is put on to the rubber when the rubber has been twisted enough.

Microfilm Model

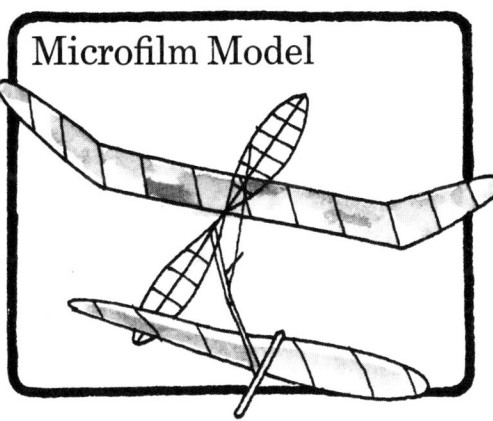

This model is made of balsa wood covered with very thin microfilm, It flies indoors and only weighs one gramme.

Simple Gliders for you to Make

If you want to try making a plane from balsa wood, you should start with a simple balsa glider which you can buy quite cheaply.

Where to Shop

If you look at the last pages of an aeromodelling magazine you will find a list of model shops. They are listed town by town so that you can go to the nearest one.

Finding out More

You should be able to find out more about model aeroplanes by writing to any of the following addresses:

Model Aeronautical Association of Australia, Hon. Sec. Gordon Burford, Witton Street, Flagstaff Hill 5179, South Australia.
Model Aeronautical Association of Canada, Box 9, Oakville, Ontario, Canada.
Model Aeronautics Council of Ireland, John McNally, Marieville, Bendermeer Park, Magazine Road, Cork.
Northern Ireland Association of Aeromodellers, Hon. Sec. Maurice Doyle, 28 Carlston Avenue, Holywood, Co. Down.
New Zealand Model Aeronautical Association, Hon. Sec. John Malkin, 51 Clyma Street, Upper Hutt.
Scottish Aeromodellers' Association, Hon. Sec. P. Malone, 105 Sighthill Loam, Edinburgh FH11 4NT.
South African Model Aeronautic Association, P.O. Box 4, Howard Place, Pinelands, Cape.
Society of Model Aeronautical Engineers, Dept MS, 116 Pall Mall, London SW1Y 5EB.

Books about Planes

How to Make and Fly Paper Aircraft	Captain Ralph S Barnaby	(Piccolo 1973)
Jet-Age Jamboree	Yasuaki Ninomiya	(Japan Publications Inc. 1968)
Aircraft	K. Munson	(MacDonald Visual Book 1971)
Aeromodeller Annuals		(Model & Allied Publications 1948)
Aeromodeller Pocket Data Book	P. G. F. Chinn	(Model & Allied Publications 1968)
Model Plane Building from A—Z	Flying Models Staff	(Carstens Publications U.S.A. 1969)
A Beginner's Guide to Building and Flying Model Aircraft	Robert Lopshire	(Harper & Row 1967)
Model Airplane Handbook	Howard McEntee	(Thomas Y Crowell U.S.A.)
Control-Line Manual	R. G. Moulton	(Model & Allied Publications 1973)
The World of Model Aircraft	Guy R Williams	(Andre Deutsch 1973)

Magazines about Planes

Aero	46, Porter Street, Prahan, Victoria 3181, Australia.
Aero Modeller	P.O. Box 35, Bridge St., Hemel Hempstead, Herts, England.
Airborne	P.O. Box 205, Blacktown 2148, Australia.
Free Flight News	11, Parkside Rd., Sunningdale, Ascot, Berks SL5 0NL, England.
Model Aeroplane Gazette	12, Slayleigh Ave., Sheffield, England.
NON News of the North	R. Magill, 1852 Great North Rd., Auckland 7, New Zealand.
Radio Modeller	64, Wellington Rd., Hampton Hill, Mddx. England.
Wings	113, Winchester House, Loveday St., Johannesburg, S. Africa.